WINK

A Modern Day Parable of Wealth Beyond Words

BY ROGER HAMILTON

WHO IS READING 'WINK'?

In its first 18 months, this book has become a bestselling book throughout South East Asia, and this is the seventh reprint. Who is reading 'Wink'?

This book has been bought by individuals looking to unlock the key to their wealth. Then many of these individuals have bought copies of this book for their friends and family. Entrepreneurs have bought this book for members of their team. Insurance and Real Estate companies have bought this book for each of their agents. Network Marketing groups have bought this book to motivate their downlines. Companies have bought this book and given it to their customers.

We have received order sizes from 1 to over 5,000. After you have read this book, decide who you know that could benefit from it. Either get them a copy, or lend them this copy. Wealth is the beginning, not the end!

Then visit us at: **www.rogerhamilton.com, www.resultsfoundation.com**

Published by Achievers International, (65) 6372 3383
Printed in Singapore by Kepmedia International Pte Ltd

ISBN 981-04-7013-4

1st published August 2002
2nd reprint December 2002
3rd reprint June 2003
4th reprint June 2004
5th reprint February 2006
6th reprint October 2006
7th reprint May 2007

“The universe is full of magical things, patiently waiting for our wits to grow sharper.”

Eden Phillpotts

Foreword

Welcome back, and thank you for reading this book.

Please be advised that this is not an ordinary story. The real story isn't in the story. The real story is a magical story behind the story, waiting to be revealed. That means it only comes out to play in a repeat reading. Whether that's in the fifth reading or the fifteenth reading is up to you.

So please use this story as you would a watering can. The more you sprinkle it, the more you grow.

Directions for use:

Apply
Rinse
Repeat

The end is in the beginning

Contents

Chapter 1

ONCE UPON A TIME

"It's just not fair!"
"I am sick and tired."

And he was. Both sick and tired. In fact, he was tired of being sick and sick of being tired. Was it fair? Richard's father had worked all his life as a carpenter. He had always wanted wealth but had never received it. That drove him to work even harder, and the pressure had finally squashed him flat.

He was flat broke, and flat on his back in bed.

"Richard, every day for the last 20 years I have visited the Well of Wealth and spent a dollar. Today, I need your help. Here's a dollar. Go buy another bucket of that Well Water, son. I'm counting on you."

Richard was nine years old. He felt sorry for his father, and a little scared. The wealth of the family now lay in his hands, with this dollar note. This dollar was the key to his family's wealth and his father's health. He held the crumpled note in both hands and listened carefully to his father's advice:

"For centuries, people in this village have made it a habit to visit the Well of Wealth every day without fail. Give generously to the Well, my son, and it will give generously to you in return."

Chapter 2

THE WELL

As Richard walked the path to the Well, he wondered why the Well hadn't given generously to his father, or to most of the other villagers for that matter. Many of them were in a worse financial state than poor dad. Sure, they got a bucket of that Well Water every day without fail. But from what he could see, all they ever did was drink it dry.

He didn't wonder for long however, as he soon came upon a fork in the road. An Old Lady sat in a deck chair relaxing in the crisp, spring air. She was holding a glass of chilled water.

Richard stopped.

"What can I do for you, young man?"

"Could you please show me the path to wealth?", Richard asked a little too loudly, holding out his dollar.

"Well, well, well! You want to be wealthy. And when will you know when you get there?"

Richard looked at the lady blankly. She smiled, and with a twinkle in her eye she added "How hard are you willing to work to become wealthy?".

"Oh, very hard! My dad has worked very hard all his life and he's still not wealthy. So I guess I'll have to work even harder than him."

"Then you'll be wanting to take this path here. Go look for the Optometrist."

Richard looked at the path. It was overgrown and uninviting compared to the other path, which was well paved and wide enough for an elephant. It reminded him of one of his father's favourite sayings:

"A man on a straight road never got lost"

But something in the Old Lady's eyes made him choose to take the overgrown path.

Before he left, she pulled out a little notebook and pen. Handing them to him, she said "Think it, ink it." She held out her other hand expectantly.

Richard looked at the dollar still in his hand. He handed it over, took the pad and scribbled down:

"Think it, ink it."

It didn't sound like anything his father had ever said. He soon found himself walking down the path, deep in the woods, looking for the Optometrist.

Chapter 3

THE OPTOMETRIST

Soon Richard came across a house in the woods. In fact, it was more like a massive mansion the size of which he had never seen before. From where he stood he could see acres of manicured gardens, beautiful fountains, a fleet of sports cars and what appeared to be a helipad on the roof, but he couldn't be sure about that last one.

He went up and knocked on the door.

A young man in a smart white frock appeared. Richard was taken aback, but quickly collected himself and thrust out his notebook. "You must be the Optometrist. The Old Lady sent me. I want to be wealthy!"

The Optometrist looked at Richard with amusement. "Well, well, well! How wealthy?"

Richard looked at him like he was an idiot. "Wealthy enough to be rich".

"Oh, that's simple! Just ask better questions."

Richard thought about this for a while, and was about to tell the Optometrist what his father thought of men in frocks, when he suddenly decided to heed the advice and ask a better question.

"So how wealthy are you?"

"I have enough income that I don't need to work, I spend my time doing what I enjoy, and I contribute to the world in ways that give me total fulfillment."

Richard looked at the man blankly.

"But how much money do you have?"

"Is that important?"

Richard crinkled his face up. He decided to change tack. "So how did you become wealthy?"

With a twinkle in his eye, the Optometrist confided, "I became a better Optometrist."

So now Richard was ready to call this whole thing off. His father had always said:

"You won't make dollars if you can't make sense."

This man seemed to be going out of his way not to make sense. But something about that twinkle reminded him of the Old Woman. He remembered the Old Woman's eyes as she sat there exclaiming "Well, well, well!".

So he asked another better question:

"And how did becoming a better Optometrist make you wealthy?"

The Optometrist took a seat on a lounge chair in his enormous reception and motioned to Richard to do the same. Richard got swallowed in the chair and couldn't help noticing that the cushions were bigger than his bed. The Optometrist began his story:

"My job is to fix people's eyesight. I specialize in children. When a child is born with imperfect eyesight they live for the first few years in a blurred world, not knowing any better. When they put on the glasses that I prescribe they will often say "So THAT'S what the world is supposed to look like!". It made me really think, because I had a feeling that I was living in a blurred world."

Richard was now getting into this idea of asking better questions. "What gave you that feeling?"

"It's not just what you ask, son. It's when you ask it. Now, as I was saying, things felt blurry. I was following the crowd, living my life. I was even visiting that Well of Wealth every day. Then several years ago I asked myself, what if I became a better optometrist in my life?"

"The answer was simple. I would have clarity. I would have focus. I would have VISION! That's when I realized I really was blurred. Because I didn't have crystal clear clarity about who I was, I didn't have a clear focus in my life. In fact, I was quite aimless, following the crowd."

"I soon realized that every great person started their journey with a great vision. They had the clarity to see where they were, and where they needed to go. Then they had the laser focus to get there. So I decided to find my vision. When I found it, my life transformed."

As the Optometrist spoke, Richard's attention had begun to wander. He wanted to know how to be wealthy. Why did he need vision as well? Surely there were wealthy people who didn't have vision. He thought about his father's vision, and that's when he sighed. His father was so short sighted he could hardly see past tomorrow.

Richard asked another question: “So you decided to work harder as a better Optometrist?”

“You really haven’t listened to me. I don’t need to work at all. My money works for me. I have investments that give me enough money to live on. I decided to BE a better Optometrist, not DO better Optometry. It wasn’t my profession that made me wealthy. It was discovering my true vision.”

“Let me show you something.” The Optometrist leaned forward and wrote on Richard’s pad:

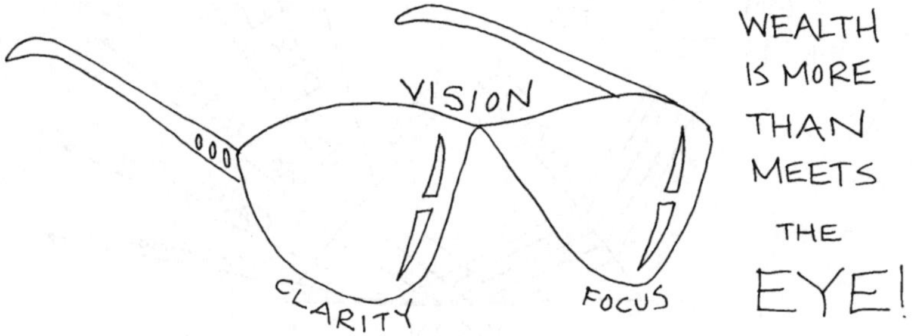

"WHAT IS YOUR QUALITY OF COMMUNICATION?"

The 4 Levels OF COMMUNICATION

1. EXCHANGE
2. CONNECT
3. MOTIVATE
4. INSPIRE

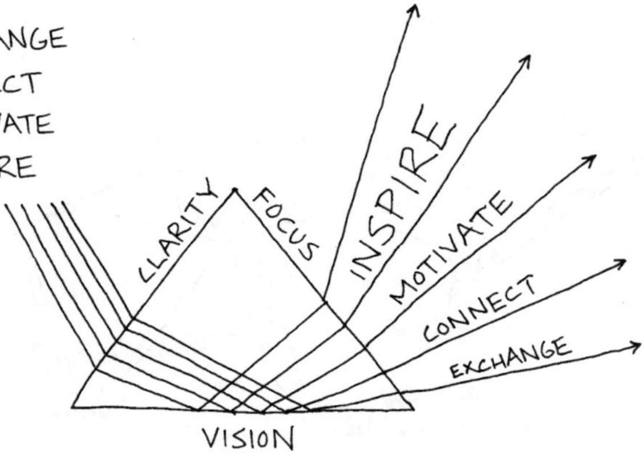

QUALITY OF COMMUNICATION = QUALITY OF LIFE

"Now, few people become wealthy in a vacuum or simply off their own resources. Your wealth will come from the time, talent, interest and resources of those around you. That means your ability to communicate will be a key to your success. There are four levels of communication, and you choose at which level you want to play."

The Optometrist pointed to the first level. "Most people simply choose to EXCHANGE, which means they can spend hours complaining or chatting without creating any clarity. People like to exchange, but no one got wealthy doing it."

He then pointed to the second level. "Some people choose to get more clarity, and when they do, they create meaning and value in their relationships. They CONNECT with those around them, which attracts more relationships and cooperation. These people are great team players and will become some of your greatest assets."

"A smaller group of people choose to become proactive with their lives, and they create a focus that others can relate to. These people are leaders. They MOTIVATE which creates connection AND momentum."

The Optometrist pointed proudly to the fourth level. "This is where I choose to play. When you INSPIRE, you become a leader of leaders. To inspire, you need vision, no doubt about it. When you play at this level, your vision becomes the cornerstone of your leadership. The key to your wealth is to learn how to lead leaders."

Richard was ready for that one. "So what was your vision?"

In response, the Optometrist did a very strange thing. He smiled, and with a twinkle in his eyes, he winked.

"What's yours?"

No one had asked Richard that before. After all, he was only nine. He realized he didn't have a vision. He didn't have much clarity or focus either. He was quite blurry.

Then he remembered the question the Old Lady had asked. He now said "If I look for my vision, how will I know when I get there?".

"When you find your vision, everything will suddenly become crystal clear. You will look around and say 'So THAT'S what the world is supposed to look like!' That is when you will begin to attract the people, the opportunities and the wealth you desire."

Richard was still skeptical. This sounded very wishy-washy to him. How could the Optometrist become wealthy just by seeing better? It wasn't that easy. He remembered his father saying:

"Money doesn't grow on trees."

And Dad should know. After all, he was a carpenter – and a good one at that. Dad could turn trees into beautiful chairs and tables. He could turn trees into wonderful door frames and window ledges. Dad could turn trees into pretty much anything, except money.

Richard thought about the Well of Wealth. That was where money came from. He asked the Optometrist "So do you still visit the Well of Wealth now that you are wealthy?".

The Optometrist laughed. "I became wealthy when I stopped visiting the Well. The Well isn't where you think it is, son. I became wealthy once I found my clarity, my focus and my vision."

"And how did you find those things?"

"You should go see the Plumber for that. That's what I did."

Richard thought about that. He felt like he was being pointed away from what he knew and accepted. He felt like he was moving further away from the Well his father had asked him to visit. He could choose to turn back now, or to continue on this journey. What would his father say? He could hear his father's words:

"Be true to yourself."

Richard looked at the Optometrist. "My father says to be true to myself. Why do I need to find a vision if I can just be true to myself?"

The Optometrist smiled. "Is your father true to himself?"

"He sure is!" Richard replied a little too defensively.

"And is he being true to his past self or his future self?"

Richard didn't like this stranger asking questions about his father, and he looked away.

"Richard, what your father says is right, but only if you see the words for what they are. If you are true to your past self, you will stay as you are. If you decide to be true to your future self, then your life will change beyond measure."

The Optometrist leaned forward and Richard looked back at him. "If you simply want to be true to your past self, a sharp memory is sufficient. However, you will be destined to remain exactly as you are today."

"If you are committed to being true to your future self, you need vision. Without it, you are on a journey without a destination. You will wander aimlessly looking for answers, only to return to what you already know. When your vision becomes stronger than your memory, your future will become more precious than your past."

Richard stood up. "OK. I'll go find this plumber. But first, I have another better question. Of all the things that you have said, what is the most useful message I can take away with me?"

The Optometrist replied:

"Your greatest asset is your vision of who you will become. Few people realize this. Invest in clarifying your vision. Once you are focused on your vision and it becomes real, this asset becomes so valuable, you can begin to trade it. Trade even a small fraction of it, and you will become as wealthy as you desire."

"Can you simplify that?"

"Sure. Choose the level you want to play at. What you see is always what you get. Learn to see better and you will get better."

Richard's eyes widened. Learn to SEE better and you will GET better! Suddenly the Optometrist had hit a chord deep inside Richard's little body. His family had gotten so little. His father had been working so hard! His father had worked so hard, he hadn't had time to think about what levels he could be playing at. He had worked so hard, he hadn't spared time to learn how to see more clearly.

If what the Optometrist said was true, every hour Richard's father spent working hard instead of learning to see better was not making them richer. It was keeping them poor.

Richard wrote this down feeling a little inspired:

"2. Choose the level you want to play at."

"3. What you see is always what you get."

Richard looked expectantly into the eyes of the Optometrist. He could see well enough to know the Optometrist was living at a different level of clarity. He could now see well enough to know that if he wanted to increase his own level, he needed to ask better questions. Richard smiled as he thought of the questions he had asked the Old Lady and the Optometrist.

He realized each of his better questions had opened another door in his journey. He wrote:

"4. Ask and you shall receive."

He thanked the frocked fellow and left to find the Plumber.

Chapter 4

THE PLUMBER

He didn't have to go far. As he was contemplating whether the Optometrist had made any sense or not, he came across a plumber knee deep in one of the fountains. He seemed to be dancing.

"You must be the Plumber. The Optometrist sent me. Can you help me become wealthy?"

The Plumber looked at Richard and said "Sure! Come in to my office".

Richard paused for a second, then took off his shoes, and holding his notebook up high, stepped in to the fountain.

"Do we need to talk in here?"

The Plumber gave him a puzzled look. "How are you going to learn about wealth if you don't know what it feels like?"

"Standing in a fountain is wealth?"

"No, but learning how to get wet without worrying is. Wealth is all around us, but most of us are too busy looking for it to notice. And when we get close, we're suddenly afraid to get wet."

Richard had a smart question to answer that. "What if I can't swim?"

"Then all the more reason to get wet and learn. You think that notebook is going to teach you to swim?"

Richard looked up at the book and replied "Think it, ink it."

The Plumber responded "Think it, ink it, do it, review it." He turned around and picked up a spanner. "Learning is a game. Remember that. Sure, plan your strokes on land, write it down, but then you've got to jump in and sink or swim. Then get back out and review what happened. Ask how you can improve. Then do it all over again. You'll learn in no time. Try to learn when you're safe and dry, and you're just kidding yourself."

Richard added to the first point on his list, and added a new point as well:

"1. Think it, ink it, do it, review it"

"5. Learning is a game"

"So what's your vision, and has it made you wealthy?"

"Sure it has. I'm a plumber. I love plumbing. My vision is to have water power generators to take over from fuel powered stations. 100% self-sustaining you know."

"And that's how you became wealthy?" Richard asked, somewhat confused.

"I became wealthy by becoming a better plumber."

Richard waited for more. This sounded like the Optometrist story already.

"I own a plumbing business. As my men service homes, I also began a maintenance and electrical services business. I have since partnered with a great manager and we franchised our services. I re-invested part of my earnings from that to launch a property development company, which is now creating double the cashflow of my franchise business."

"About 40% of the monthly cashflow I draw out of my businesses covers my expenses, and the rest goes into investments. I also put 20% into my pet project, Water Generators."

The plumber seemed to have a lot of clarity and focus. But Richard couldn't fathom how his vision had made him wealthy. In fact, it seemed to be costing him. But before he got to that, he had a more immediate remark he wanted to make: "It sounds like you became wealthy by being a better businessman, not a better plumber."

The plumber laughed. "I have no passion for business. I have a passion for plumbing. I became a better plumber."

Richard offered a confused look.

"I will elaborate. Plumbing comes naturally to me. I can solve plumbing problems. I love plumbing. When it came to money-making, management and other such business-like things I always lost interest. Bored me silly."

"Then I decided to BE a better plumber. I took my passion and spread it to areas of my life that were important to me. Being wealthy was important, so when I looked at my wealth creation as a simple plumbing system, I took to it with a passion. It was fun! It's got to be fun, son."

He sat on the side of the fountain, and began to draw in Richard's pad. He drew:

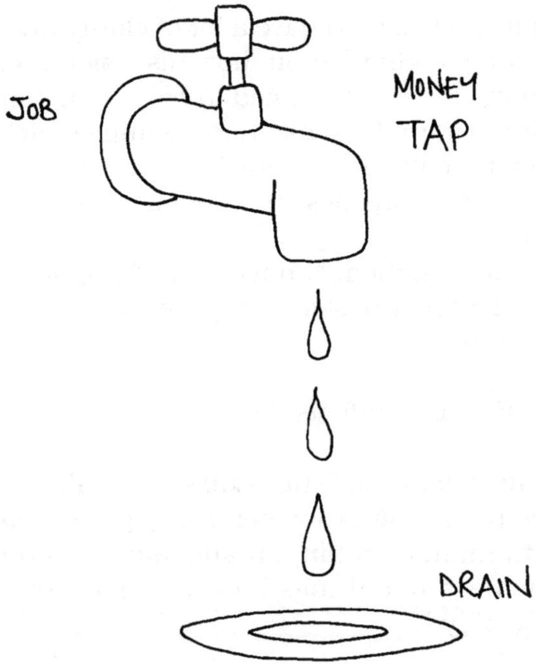

"Now, what I realized was, no matter how much money I was making, it was always disappearing. This was my money tap, and all the money was going down the drain. I was spending it all, and as a bad plumber all I could think to do was to try and open the tap up further. It just meant more went down the drain."

To Richard, that sounded like his father. It also sounded like what happened to all those buckets of water from the Well of Wealth.

"So as a better plumber, I diverted some of that money into savings. All that did was fill a bucket with water, but not much else. Then as an even better plumber, I diverted some of that money into investments. While my savings just sat in a bucket, my investments created new money taps. My money began to make money."

"It soon became obvious to me that every drop spent never came back and every drop invested and re-invested began to give me ever increasing returns. As a good plumber, I simply ensured that an ever-increasing percentage of my cashflow was going into investments. That meant investment in my businesses, in my people, and in myself. I began with 10% of my cashflow, and after three years that had grown to 40%, and after six years it was up to 60%."

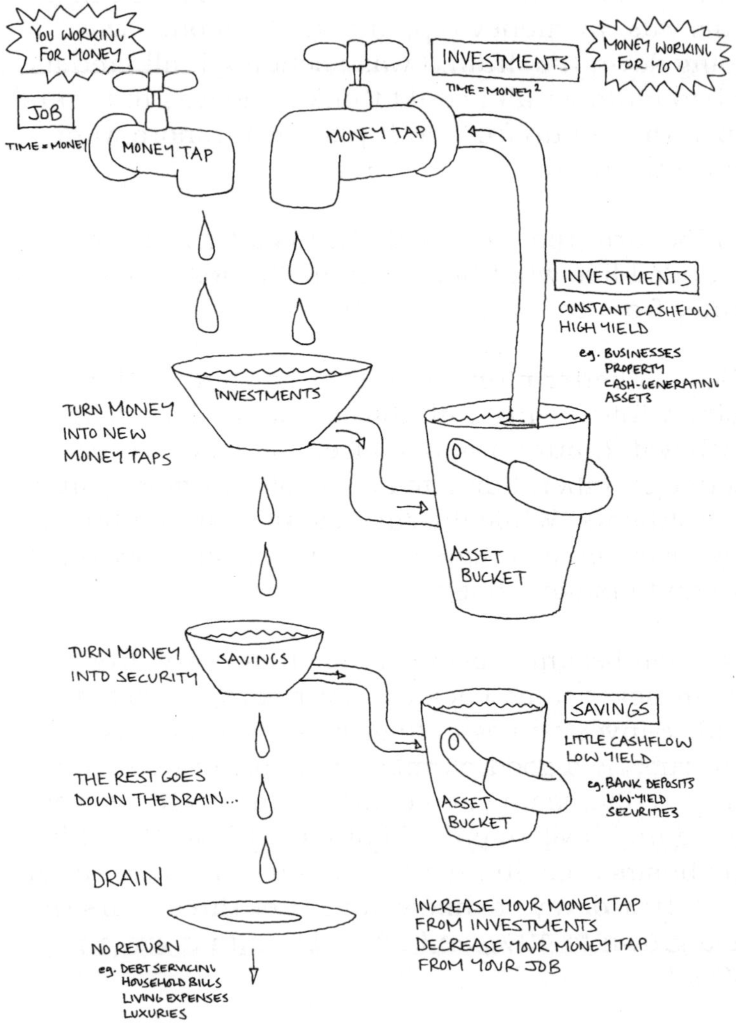
YOU WORKING FOR MONEY
JOB
TIME = MONEY
MONEY TAP
INVESTMENTS
TIME = MONEY²
MONEY WORKING FOR YOU
MONEY TAP
INVESTMENTS
CONSTANT CASHFLOW
HIGH YIELD
eg. BUSINESSES
PROPERTY
CASH-GENERATING
ASSETS
INVESTMENTS
TURN MONEY INTO NEW MONEY TAPS
ASSET BUCKET
TURN MONEY INTO SECURITY
SAVINGS
SAVINGS
LITTLE CASHFLOW
LOW YIELD
eg. BANK DEPOSITS
LOW-YIELD
SECURITIES
ASSET BUCKET
THE REST GOES DOWN THE DRAIN...
DRAIN
NO RETURN
eg. DEBT SERVICING
HOUSEHOLD BILLS
LIVING EXPENSES
LUXURIES
INCREASE YOUR MONEY TAP FROM INVESTMENTS
DECREASE YOUR MONEY TAP FROM YOUR JOB

"My money tap from my investments and businesses also outgrew my money tap from my own efforts. So I could stop working in my business, and start working on it. Of course, none of that would have happened if I hadn't decided to become a better plumber."

Richard wasn't so easily convinced. He knew his Dad saved a little each month and tried to re-invest. But he wasn't making much money to start with, and he seemed to lose as much on his investments as he made.

"I can understand how your plumbing system works if you have something coming out of your money tap. But what if it only trickles out, like my Dad's. It would take forever for him to fill his investment bucket and start another money tap. Even then, it would only drip."

The plumber gave a big wide smile. "So give me a better question."

Richard thought. He had told the Old Lady he was willing to work hard, but he wasn't expecting it to be this kind of hard work. He thought harder.

"How can I create a money tap with no money?"

"Very good. You start with another tap of something more valuable than money."

"Er...Gold?"

"Time. We all have the same time coming out of the time tap. Ironically, those who value money over their time will never become wealthy. Those who value their time over money, attract wealth in no time."

Richard thought about that without really understanding it. He sat, ready to write something important down.

"I found that I was SPENDING my money instead of INVESTING it. I also found that I was spending my TIME, instead of investing it. Most of us do. Most of my time was going straight down the drain in low value activities. So I created a better plumbing system." He drew his plumbing system.

"Now, 24 drops come out of this tap every day. If you spend that time on activities that do not add any value to your life other than to make you feel good temporarily or to pass the time, those are drops spent. They are gone and they ain't ever coming back."

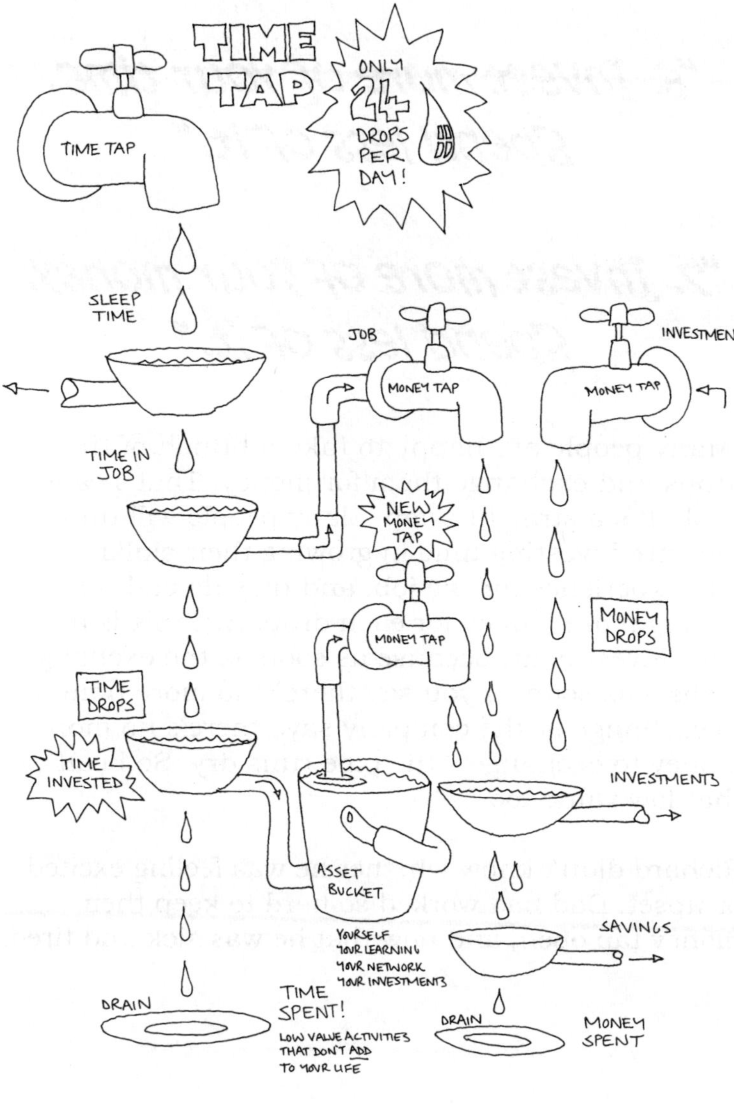
TIME TAP
ONLY 24 DROPS PER DAY!
TIME TAP
SLEEP TIME
TIME IN JOB
JOB
MONEY TAP
INVESTMENTS
MONEY TAP
NEW MONEY TAP
MONEY TAP
MONEY DROPS
TIME DROPS
TIME INVESTED
ASSET BUCKET
YOURSELF
YOUR LEARNING
YOUR NETWORK
YOUR INVESTMENTS
INVESTMENTS
SAVINGS
DRAIN
TIME SPENT!
LOW VALUE ACTIVITIES THAT DON'T ADD TO YOUR LIFE
DRAIN
MONEY SPENT

Richard suddenly realized that most of his time had been spent and he wrote:

"6. Invest more of your time. Spend less of it."

"7. Invest more of your money. Spend less of it."

"Many people are happy to take a bunch of their drops and exchange them for money. That's called a job. It's a straight swap. Many people will think they are investing time in growing their skills and experience for the job, and they do end up getting more money for each drop. But this is a false investment, because as soon as the exchange stops – as soon as you say there's no more time to exchange or the company says there's no more money to exchange – the pipe runs dry. So I call that low value too."

Richard didn't know whether he was feeling excited or upset. Dad had worked so hard to keep their money tap open, and now that he was sick and tired, their money tap had run dry. The reward for all his effort was a tired body and a sore head.

The Plumber continued. “So as a better plumber, I began to divert my time drops to high value use – to investments of time. Every drop invested here gives me on going returns, for life! Because it is here that your time creates new money taps AND creates new time taps!”

Richard interrupted, “But how do you know if you are spending time or investing time?”

“When you spend your time, you may have gotten something, but you haven’t built anything. When you invest your time, you end that day or that week having built something that is lasting. I’ll show you what I mean.”

He added to his plumbing diagram.

“When you invest your time in yourself, it is time invested on your health, on quality activities that enrich your life. New experiences and greater energy and vitality that make you stronger every day.”

Richard suddenly realized that the reason his father was sick and tired was because he had this pipe permanently closed. His father thought exercise and trying new things were a waste of time. So he had chosen to close that pipe. Now, he didn't have money and he had also exhausted his time.

"When you invest in your learning, I'm not talking about learning how to DO better plumbing. I'm talking about learning how to BE a better plumber. Learn the strategies, habits and mindset of the wealthy - because it is a different mindset."

"Learn how to change your level of focus and clarity. Learn what your vision is. That's real time investment. It's what you're doing right now."

Richard thought about that as he held his book. Had he thought of this as an investment of his time? Either way, his toes were starting to wrinkle in the water.

"When you invest in your network, you are creating and building your network of friends, peers and contacts. The time you invest looking after your network will all return with interest. You never know when you will need the support of the people you know, and of the people that they know. Your influence is only as good as your network."

"When you invest in your investments, which means your cash investments, property and your businesses, I'm not talking about spending time working in them. I'm talking about investing your time in choosing your investments and creating your businesses, in building

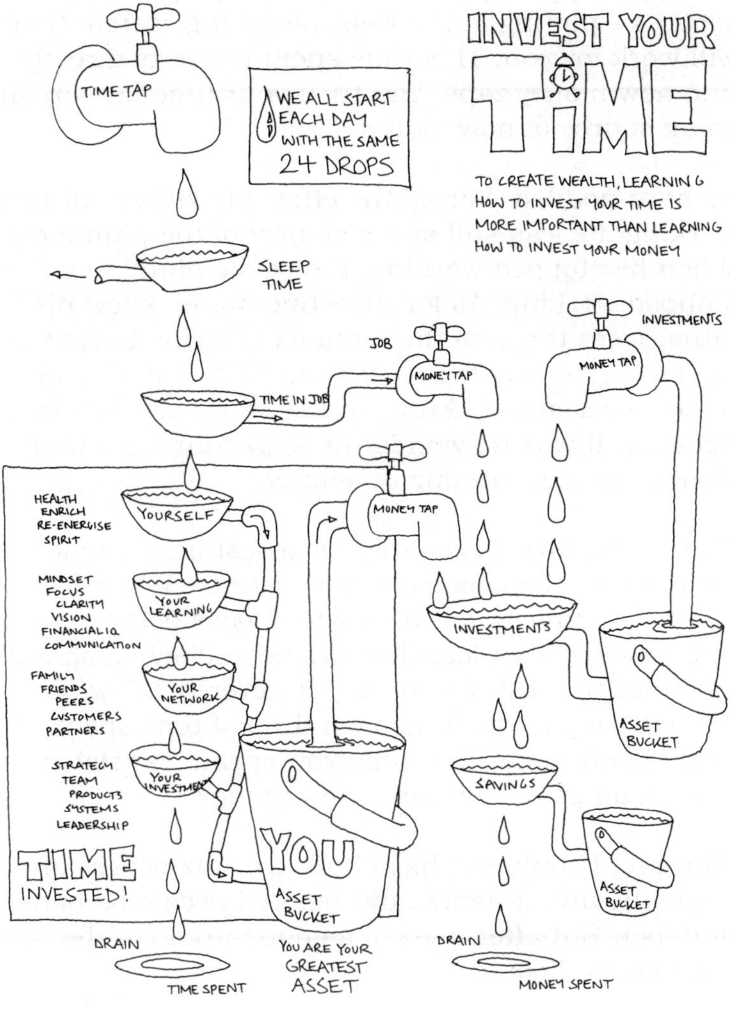
INVEST YOUR TIME
TO CREATE WEALTH, LEARNING HOW TO INVEST YOUR TIME IS MORE IMPORTANT THAN LEARNING HOW TO INVEST YOUR MONEY
TIME TAP
WE ALL START EACH DAY WITH THE SAME 24 DROPS
SLEEP TIME
TIME IN JOB
JOB
MONEY TAP
INVESTMENTS
MONEY TAP
HEALTH
ENRICH
RE-ENERGISE
SPIRIT
YOURSELF
MINDSET
FOCUS
CLARITY
VISION
FINANCIAL IQ
COMMUNICATION
YOUR LEARNING
FAMILY
FRIENDS
PEERS
CUSTOMERS
PARTNERS
YOUR NETWORK
STRATEGY
TEAM
PRODUCTS
SYSTEMS
LEADERSHIP
YOUR INVESTMENT
TIME INVESTED!
MONEY TAP
YOU
ASSET BUCKET
INVESTMENTS
ASSET BUCKET
SAVINGS
ASSET BUCKET
DRAIN
TIME SPENT
YOU ARE YOUR GREATEST ASSET
DRAIN
MONEY SPENT

them. Investing your time in selecting the right people, the right opportunities, the right products and services – putting in the right plumbing system that will work for you. This time spent converts directly into new money taps. You turn your time into an on going source of new money."

Richard nodded. For all the effort his father put into working, he was still stuck as part of the plumbing. When he stopped working, the whole plumbing stopped working. As for investments, he knew his father went through the motions of trying to save money and trying to invest some of it, but he had really never invested time in his knowledge or his network. It was no wonder he kept running out of steam. He was running on empty.

"When you invest time in your investments, time isn't money. Time is more than money. When you invest time to learn how to choose better investments, that learning can be applied again and again for the rest of your life. It never goes away. The return you get from each drop of time spent here is enormous. The time you spend translates into an on going stream of new money."

"You see, I could not have built the businesses and made the investments I did before I became a better plumber. But after investing enough time in the right areas, I could."

The Plumber paused for effect, and then said "Show me how a man spends and invests his time, and I will show you his future."

Richard drew a pie of how he had been spending and investing his time. It depressed him. He then drew one for his father.

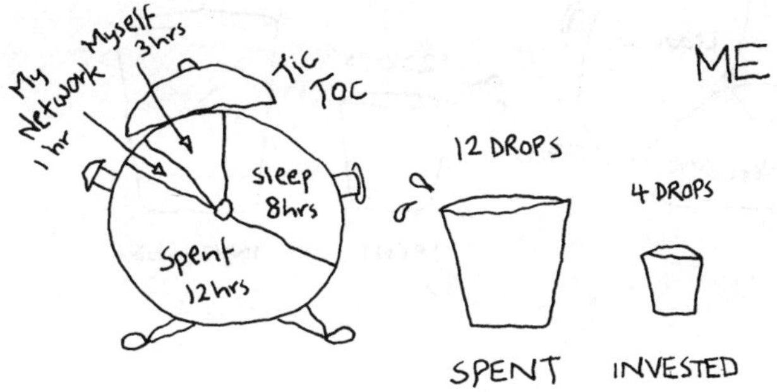

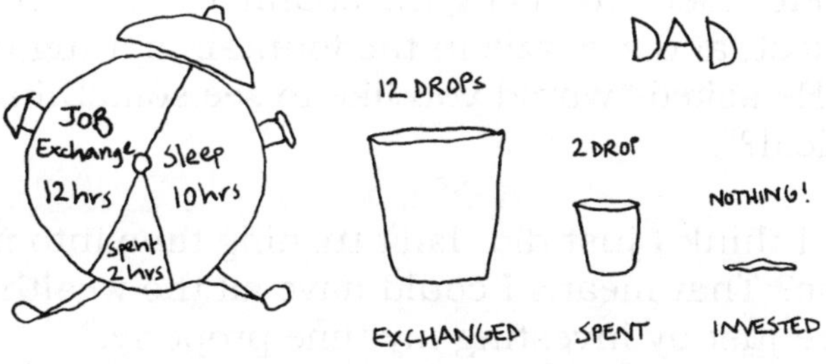

It was at that point that the boy realized he had increased his clarity enormously. He really was learning. He drew a pie of how he had spent his time today:

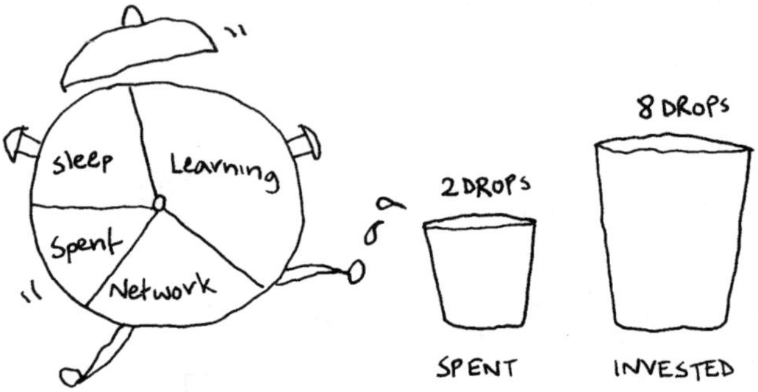

The Plumber was using the spanner to loosen a faucet, and a nozzle in the fountain sprang to life. He asked "Would you like to see something magical?".

"But I think I just did. Isn't turning time into money magic? That means I could have all the wealth I desire just by investing my time properly."

"Sure, that's magic. It's also good plumbing. Now, go see the Gardener."

"Thank you, but before I go, I have a question. Is the time and money spent on your vision an investment if you don't get a return? And how has your vision made you wealthy?"

"Well, well, well!" smiled the plumber. "Your questions are getting better. But this time, I think you already have the answer."

Richard left a little confused. If he had the answer, why couldn't he see it. He remembered what the optician said, and decided to reread it:

"3. What you see is always what you get."

He decided he was going to have to work even harder than he had promised the Old Lady.

Chapter 5

THE GARDENER

Finding the Gardener wasn't difficult. Richard followed the lawn down to a river, and on the banks lay the most beautiful exhibition of flowers, hedges and fruit trees he had ever seen. An equally beautiful lady sat under a mango tree having a picnic with two girls.

"Hello, I'm Richard. I have just been speaking with the Plumber. Could you show me something magical?"

The Gardener smiled. "Richard. Hmmm. So which is it?"

"Pardon?"

"Rich-hard. Your name. So which is it? Is life Rich? Or is life Hard?"

What a strange question. Without thinking, Richard said "Life is hard... Isn't it?"

It was probably one of the silliest things he could have said.

Here he was, sitting in this beautiful garden, in the warm summer sun, looking over a gentle river, feeling totally at peace. How could he possibly think life is hard? But he did, because he always had, like his father always had.

The warmth of the day enveloped him. He was surprised to feel a shiver. Something was about to happen. As he looked over the beauty surrounding him, his lips moved and he heard his father's voice "Life IS hard."

The Gardener sat like she was listening to some wonderful music in the air. Then from her smiling breath came a whispered melody "Well, well, well..."

The shiver turned into a spine tingling revelation. Richard's eyes widened and began to water.

"Well, well, well."

And then he saw the magic all at once.

It caught his breath.

"Well, well, well."

It really was magic. It was all around him. It had

been there all day and he hadn't seen it. Now, all of a sudden, he was seeing more clearly. What he saw stunned him. It was totally overwhelming.

He was looking directly into the Well of Wealth.

With deep breaths, he began to skim through the words the Old Lady, the Optician, the Plumber and the Gardener had been using. He began remembering what each of them had been saying, remembering what he had begun asking, what he had begun writing.

He spun round to face the Gardener with a look of exhilaration in his eyes. She could see that he could see it. He laughed out loud and shouted "Well, well, well!"

He jumped up and danced across the garden, amusing the two girls, "Well, well, well! It's the Well of Wealth! You all know it already! Anyone can see it, but most of us don't! I never saw it. But I can see it now! The Well is in our Words!"

"THE WELL IS IN OUR WORDS!!"

He sat back on the bench, wiping the tears from his eyes. "I didn't mean what I said. I really didn't mean it. Life isn't hard. Life is Rich. I really believe life is Rich, and it is Richer than I ever imagined."

The Gardener added “Life is Hard or Life is Rich – what you see is always what you get.” Then she echoed “The Well is in your Words”.

Richard spoke with a tingle of excitement, “I could feel that the people I’ve met today think differently from my father and the people I know in the village. They use different words and they ask better questions. I thought that they could ask better questions because they have a better mindset. But now I know I had it all upside down.”

“They have a better mindset because they asked better questions. Because they used better words.”

“As you are doing now!” the Gardener added.

Richard continued, “The Plumber, the Optician. They started just like me, just like my father. But when they started changing their words, they started growing their clarity. They began to tap into the Well and that’s why they are now wealthy.”

“All our lives, we have been visiting the Well of Wealth. But it’s not the real Well at all. The real Well is in our Words, and it is so much bigger than I ever imagined.”

The Gardener nodded, "And every Word of Wealth that you speak or think taps in to the Well. Every better question that you ask draws from the Well. It's limitless."

"It's magic!" Richard wrote:

"8. Your Well is in your Words."

The Gardener smiled again. She then looked at Richard and did something peculiar. With the most enchanting twinkle in her eye, she winked.

Richard remembered what the plumber had said:

"5. Learning is a game"

He was beginning to really enjoy this game.

"Are you wealthy?"

"I have two wonderful daughters and an incredible husband, I have my health and I have my time, so yes, I am wealthy."

"Do you have businesses and investments giving you money taps so you don't have to worry about money?"

"All the land you see here. I own it. The Optometrist pays me rent, as do eighty-five other wealthy residents in the area. I also have investments in a number of property developments in the village.

"I used to earn simply as a gardener, but I put some of my earnings aside and more importantly I invested my time in becoming very convincing in front of financiers and bankers. I also invested my time to meet and learn from successful land and property developers."

"I had a vision to own my own piece of mother nature, you see. My vision was that nature would give me my wealth, and I would give my wealth to nature in return. That's what a good gardener does. That's what you see here. I'm living my dream."

The girls were now playing pat-a-cake by the river. Richard suddenly became aware of the warmth of the sun. He noticed that they were not alone. There were colorful birds chattering in the trees and a rainbow of butterflies playing in the flowerbeds. Richard felt a knot in his stomach as he thought of their little home and his dad, sick and tired in bed.

Richard thought for a moment. "But if the Optometrist is so wealthy, why is he renting his house from you?"

"The Optometrist has an incredible vision. In his vision it doesn't make sense for him to tie his money up in a permanent home. He prefers to invest his money, and treat his home as an expense. And besides, this way I'm happy to garden for him. He loves my gardening."

Even though he knew the answer, Richard asked the next question anyway. "And how did you get so wealthy?"

The gardener laughed at the river. "I became a better gardener!"

"As you've been with the Plumber, I can imagine what you have learnt. So what is your better question?"

Richard was ready. "I know I need to find my vision, and I know I need to invest my time instead of spending it. But how?"

"A better question, if you please?"

Richard had a question at the back of his mind that didn't seem relevant but then maybe it was. "The plumber didn't need to work. Neither do you. So why do you?"

"Nice question! To me, gardening isn't my work. It's my passion. Every moment gardening I'm fulfilling my vision. That's the secret, Richard. Your wealth starts in your mind. Wealth isn't the end. It's the beginning."

"How was wealth the beginning for you?"

"Do you see this garden? It's a wealth of color and scents and sounds. It began as a patch of ground. I gave it a wealth of water, sun, care, attention and passion. In return I have a wealth of nature that gives back to me every day. The wealth began long before the flowers bloomed."

Richard sat looking at the flowers, and he smiled at those words. The wealth began long before the flowers bloomed.

He wrote down:

"9. Wealth is the beginning, not the end."

"I see how you got clarity. But how did you get focus?"

"When I decided to become a better gardener, I minimized the time I spent and I maximized the time I invested. I treated my life as a garden, and my focus was like my garden hose. What I focused on was watered and grew. What I did not focus on dried and died."

Richard thought about all the weeds in his father's garden that were constantly focused on. Every time his father said "It's not fair" he had watered and grown that weed into an enormous tree. Even worse, all the gifts and aspirations had been neglected, and had shriveled. He took a breath.

"I soon realized that my highest value activities were sowing, nurturing and reaping. This was true for my learning, for my network and for my investments. I had little experience or interest in finance, but I had plenty of experience and interest in gardening.

"I sowed the seeds in every new person I met and in every new tool I learnt to use. I nurtured my relationships and my investments. I reaped the rewards consciously and when the time was right. If I had not, I am likely to have tried to reap too early, not sown with enough care or not nurtured with enough commitment.

"I became wealthy simply by becoming a better gardener."

Richard thought hard about himself and his father. What had they sown? What had they nurtured? No wonder they hadn't grown very much. What was there to grow when they hadn't taken the time to sow anything?

He asked out loud "So is visiting the Well of Wealth sowing or reaping?"

"Which Well?" the Gardener laughed.

"Not the real Well - not the Well in our Words. The one the villagers visit every day."

"Well then I think you already know that it's neither."

Richard thought about the plumber's time tap. He already knew that he had to invest his time instead of spending it. Now he understood that he needed to split his time investment into sowing, nurturing and reaping.

He wrote:

"10. Sow, nurture, reap."

It was then that he suddenly realized he had been missing a tremendous opportunity to sow. He had met all these fantastic people, and he hadn't asked to keep in touch with them. He immediately decided to do so, starting with the Gardener: "Could we be friends?"

"If that's what you would like. Sure, I'd happy to be your friend."

What did she mean, 'If that's what I would like'? Richard knew he was missing something. He had to work harder on his better questions. He watched the girls, who had decided to go for a swim in the river. He wondered what the fish thought of that.

He asked "As you grew your garden, how did you know what to focus on?"

"Have you heard the expression 'Can't see the wood for the trees'? Until I knew what I wanted my garden to look like, I didn't know what to focus on. Once I had a vision, once I had a clear picture of what my garden would look like, I could begin to see what I needed to sow, what I needed to nurture, what I needed to reap. When I wandered through my garden each day, it was clear to me where I should invest my 24 drops of water. With only 24 drops, I had to be careful where I invested it.

THE GARDENER'S GARDEN
PROPERTIES
BUSINESSES
TEAM
ADVISORS
PARTNERS
INVESTORS
FINANCIAL IQ
FOCUS
WEALTH MINDSET
CLARITY
LEADERSHIP
VISION
COMMUNICATION
TEACHERS
MENTORS
FRIENDS
INSPIRED WORKS IN PROGRESS
FAMILY
PEERS

"And you know something? Day after day I began to see the old roots and weeds wither as I neglected them. I began to see my learning, my friendships, my contacts and my investments flourish. My daily walk through my garden was always exciting and fun.

"So, Richard. Tell me, what do you want your garden to look like?"

Richard was no gardener. He had once tried to grow a potato in a small pot at home, but that was about it. But he was inspired listening to the Gardener, and he remembered what the Optician had said about the four levels of communication:

"2. Choose the level you want to play at."

"I want to have a beautiful garden too. I want to see more than the trees. I want to be able to see the wood for the trees. I really want to see the wood. I want to live an inspiring life, where wealth is returned from the wealth that I give. I want to live with my own great vision. How do I find it?"

"If you want to find your vision, follow your passion. The less your work feels like work, the closer you are getting."

Richard began to feel the blur returning. "The Plumber never mentioned anything about passion."

"Then you weren't listening. From what I know, that's all he ever mentions. If you seek your vision, let passion be your compass. Now there's someone I would like you to meet."

Richard got to his feet and followed the Gardener down to the riverbank. As he walked he wrote:

"11. Your passion is your compass."

He thought about his father again. His passion was complaining. So how was that going to make them wealthy?

They found the girls by a fishing boat, docked by the bank. A bearded man was showing them a fat fish, which he then handed to them. They threw it back in the water with a squeal and started giggling in a way that reminded Richard of his mum.

"Richard, I would like you to meet the Fisherman. Richard is a young man seeking the wood."

Richard thrust out his hand. "Hello, I'm Richard. At your service!"

"Well, well, well!" exclaimed the Fisherman. "After the wood, are you? Well then hop in, we're going down stream."

Richard jumped in and turned to the Gardener. "If you were to give me your best words of wisdom, what would they be?"

The Gardener looked around her paradise with a sigh, and then spoke to her daughters. "Girls, why don't you give Richard something to take with him?"

One of the girls looked at Richard, and he noticed for the first time her beautiful eyes. They twinkled. As the Fisherman cast off, she sang

"The World is waiting,
Anticipating..."

Richard kept eye contact for as long as he dared? as he felt his heart pounding.

Chapter 6

THE FISHERMAN

The Fisherman roared with laughter. "She's right there, lad. It's a waiting game. The World waits for us to give, while we wait for the World to give. It's a waiting game alright."

"Isn't fishing a waiting game?"

"Oh, it was, until I became a better fisherman."

"And what wealth do you have?"

"I own a retail chain. You see what I wear? These boots? This jacket? From my chain. Fine material. I like to spend time with my people. Like I spend time here with the fish. That's what I love. That's the wealth that I have. How about you?"

"I don't have much wealth."

The Fisherman whistled "The World is waiting, anticipating...". Then he said with a start "Are you blind, boy?", knocking the side of the boat with a loud rap.

Richard had a sudden wave of seasickness – even though there was no sea. Or maybe it was just uncertainty. He looked at the Fisherman with his notebook ready.

"You want to find the wood? Could, should, wood. Here's the wood. It's right here. It's all around you. You're sitting in it."

He rapped the boat again.

Richard couldn't help noticing that the boat looked pretty worn for someone who was supposed to be wealthy.

"No, the Gardener meant – I meant – the wood from the trees. I'm looking for the wood from the trees. My vision."

The Fisherman changed subject. "I'll show you how to be a better fisherman if you promise to focus on catching a fish."

"Sure," Richard said, notebook poised.

"Then, here." The Fisherman stopped the engine and pulled out a fishing rod. He handed it to Richard. "Start fishing."

Richard started "I didn't know you meant really catch a fish. Can't you just explain it to me? Why do I need to catch a fish?"

"You'd better start asking better questions, lad. The first reason you've got that rod is because to know and not to do, is not yet to know. The second reason is because it's coming up to lunchtime and I'm hungry."

Richard took the rod, and with his other hand he wrote down:

"12. To know and not to do, is not yet to know."

The more he was learning, the more he seemed not to know. So he decided it was time to start doing more. He put his notebook down and asked "What should I use to catch the fish?"

"You choose." The Fisherman presented a case of beautiful multi-coloured fishing flies. As Richard looked at the selection, he immediately saw the one he liked best. "I'll take that one."

The Fisherman didn't move. He just sat there looking out at the river.

Richard waited a moment. Then asked "Which one works best?"

"Oh, I thought you would never ask. This one here." He picked out a fly that, quite frankly, looked like a three-legged grasshopper. Richard wasn't about to argue.

The Fisherman connected the fly. "Now stand up, stretch the rod back like this, and..."

The line went flying forward and the fly landed far downstream. "Now start to gently reel it back in." Richard did, and was shocked when within moments the line went taut. He kept reeling in, using more strength. In his moment of need, the Fisherman left him and went down to his cabin below deck.

"Mr. Fisherman!" Richard yelled as the fish came up to the surface, "Help!"

The Fisherman returned with a basket, and pulled the fish out of the water by the line. "Hello, Sally! Good to see you again. Say hello to Richard." He gave the fish a nod in Richard's direction, then cut her loose and dropped her back in the water. Sally splashed away.

"You know that fish?"

"Just a little joke of mine. Sally's my wife. Now, time for lunch."

He pulled open the basket to present a spread of sandwiches, fruit and desserts.

"I thought you wanted to eat the fish for lunch."

"No, plenty more fish in the sea as they say. Or in the river on this occasion. So here endeth the lesson on how to be a better fisherman. Now you need to live up to your end of the bargain, and commit to catching a fish."

"But I just did!" Richard protested.

"I mean a real fish. A money tap. No point knowing if there ain't no doing."

Richard took a sandwich. "How did you start your first money tap?"

"As I said, I became a better fisherman. I used to think ABOUT the fish. When I became a better fisherman, I began to think LIKE the fish. It's different, you know. I was out chasing the fish, which is never ending. I was a sales manager at the time, and I hated my job - simply because it was never ending. Continually chasing customers.

"When I became a better fisherman, I focused on creating a better fly. Surely I could make one that would be more attractive. When you create attraction, you never have to chase again. So I invested my time on creating value. There's no wealth where there's no value. Value is the river in which Wealth flows."

Richard wrote that down as he continued to listen:

"13. Value is the river in which Wealth flows."

"I looked outside of my job at other products that people seemed to be attracted to. I was selling outdoor jackets that just didn't have the demand in the market at the time. So I invested my own time to learn more about what people were buying. That meant I also met the traders who were being a lot more successful than me.

"After only six months I had enough knowledge and contacts to begin my own retail store where I chose the clothing ranges that I knew would sell. And then every day I added more value to the customer and to my vendors. Every day I asked myself how much more value I could provide.

I became an inspired work-in-progress. The store was so successful that a chain of stores soon followed."

"What do you mean by an inspired work-in-progress?"

The Fisherman picked up the fly. "You see this? It may look like it only took five minutes to make, but it really took five years. Every day I would think of a better fly, design it, see how it worked, and then try again."

Richard remembered what the Plumber had said:

"1. Think it, ink it, do it, review it"

"So this fly is an inspired work-in-progress. Because it's still not perfect. It never will be, because that would spoil the fun. The fun is in the trial and error. So that's me too. I'm an inspired work-in-progress."

Richard thought about the Gardener's garden, and the Plumber's vision. They were very inspired works-in-progress. He added that to his list:

"14. Become an inspired work-in-progress."

"But when you started your store, weren't you afraid that you might fail?"

"Hell no, I planned to fail! You have to plan to fail, lad, or you will be constantly disappointed. Have a look out here." The Fisherman gestured at the river like he was conducting an orchestra. "In this river there are a thousand fish. When I sink my line, I am planning to fail to catch all but one of them, which means I am planning for a failure rate of 99.9%. If that failure rate becomes 99.8%, I will have caught two fish, which will have doubled my results for the day."

"When I experiment with new marketing ideas, or new store promotions, or new product lines, I always invest my time and money with the expectation of a high failure rate, and I ensure that with this high rate I can still get a reasonable return on my time and money invested. So day by day I learn profitably."

"Have you ever had results worse than expected?"

"Sure I have. Before I became a better fisherman it happened all the time. I would always set high expectations and high targets, and I was constantly disappointed. Worse, I would budget my time and money on the basis of my high expectations. So as well as being disappointed, time and money that I thought I was investing became wasted."

"Now that I have become a better fisherman, I plan to fail. So most of the time I am pleasantly surprised by the results. But I still face bigger failures than expected, and these I welcome. Because each failure is a new opportunity to make an even better fly."

Richard was inspired. The Fisherman had failed many, many times more than his father, and that is how he had become so successful. And he was having fun doing it.

For the Fisherman, learning really was a game. Richard couldn't help thinking that maybe few people played because they didn't know the rules.

The Fisherman seemed to know what Richard was thinking and he said:

"Plan to be wealthy by failing nine times out of ten. That way, whether you are succeeding or failing, you will still be wealthy. If you plan to be wealthy by succeeding nine times out of ten, wealth will always elude you – unless, of course, you get lucky. Some fishermen do that, you know. They wait to get lucky. For them, it's a waiting game alright."

Richard wrote down:

"15. Plan to fail."

The river began to widen and the stream continued to slow. The Fisherman put up his feet and said "Now I have a question for you. What was it that you learnt, that made you a better fisherman?"

Richard was about to answer, when he stopped himself. He didn't do much except throw in the line and reel in the fish. In fact, he had started by picking the wrong fly. Then he remember asking the Fisherman which one worked best, and he remembered what he had written after meeting the Optometrist:

"4. Ask and you shall receive."

"I learnt to ask when I didn't know."

"When you didn't know or when you didn't want to invest the time in finding out?"

"Well, I certainly wouldn't want to invest five years finding out."

"And in such a situation who should you ask?"

Richard smiled, "I would ask an inspired work-in-progress who had a passion about such a thing as fly fishing."

"Exactly. You can accelerate your progress tremendously by investing your time in a network that includes many inspired works-in-progress. That's what all wealthy people do, you know. That way, you invest your own time in learning that directly supports your own passion and vision."

Richard tried to clarify this. "So you decided to be an inspired work-in-progress in creating value because that is where your passion and vision is. Then you would find people like the Plumber to create a better plumbing system and the Gardener to create a better garden, because that is where their passion and vision is?"

"Exactly!"

"But why would you help me?"

"Because I know an inspired work-in-progress when I see one."

Richard was starting to feel very good about himself. But he was anxious that he was still not doing enough. He asked the Fisherman:

"What can I do to be wealthy today?"

The Fisherman chuckled. "They don't make nine year olds like they used to." He rapped the side of the boat again. "See the wood, lad. That's where you'll find your wealth." He pointed the boat to the bank, and Richard turned to see a boathouse.

Chapter 7

THE ROWER

The Fisherman docked by the jetty, and a rower carrying a racing scull approached. "This is the end of the line, lad. I'm going in for a pint of bitter. Call me when you are ready. And remember your promise!"

Richard watched him walk towards the boathouse. Call him when I'm ready? Ready for what? Richard felt he was already ready for anything. But he was clearly not. There was something very big that he was not seeing. He watched the Rower put his scull in the water, and lock in the oars.

Richard looked at the Rower, and realized he should be getting back. He put out his hand and without thinking said:

"Hello, I'm Rich. Can you help me?"

The Rower laughed. "Well, if you're rich shouldn't you be asking how you can help me?"

Richard reddened in embarrassment. "OK. How can I help you?"

The Rower leaned back on a mooring. "I've got an hour of rowing ahead of me. Inspire me."

Richard began his story. "My father was sick today. He is sick a lot. Sick and tired. I'm his only son, and I love him. He is so gifted and he doesn't even know it. I help him in his work and I know how good he is. I'm going to make sure we invest our time and build a better plumbing system, to grow a beautiful garden."

"I'm going to go home today and create a life where we attract the wealth we deserve, and the time we deserve. The time together, because there's nothing more precious than time, and there's nothing more valuable to me than the time I have with my Dad. It isn't the biggest life but it's my life and it's going to be fantastic."

"Great story! I can see that. Nice vision."

Rich gaped at the man. His eyes watered like he had just opened them for the first time. He spun around and stared at the Fisherman's boat, with crystal clarity, then he ran towards the boathouse. He ran so fast he was tripping over his feet. He was ready.

"I'm ready! I can help you!"

The Fisherman looked up and smiled.

"Sorry I was a little slow, but I'm learning! I'm an inspired work-in-progress! Your boat: I'll sand and polish the wood. I've done it for my father many times. He's a carpenter."

"Ah, so you finally saw the wood!"

"When the Gardener said 'Can't see the Wood for the Trees', I heard it the way I had always heard it. The Wood was the big picture – the vision. And I know that it is, but I only just realized that the Wood also means what can be created from the trees. That opportunities can be created out of every moment."

The Fisherman nodded. "I like that, you should write that down."

Rich pulled out the notebook and wrote:

"16. See the Wood from the Trees."

"17. Opportunities lie in every moment."

In a moment of inspiration he also drew:

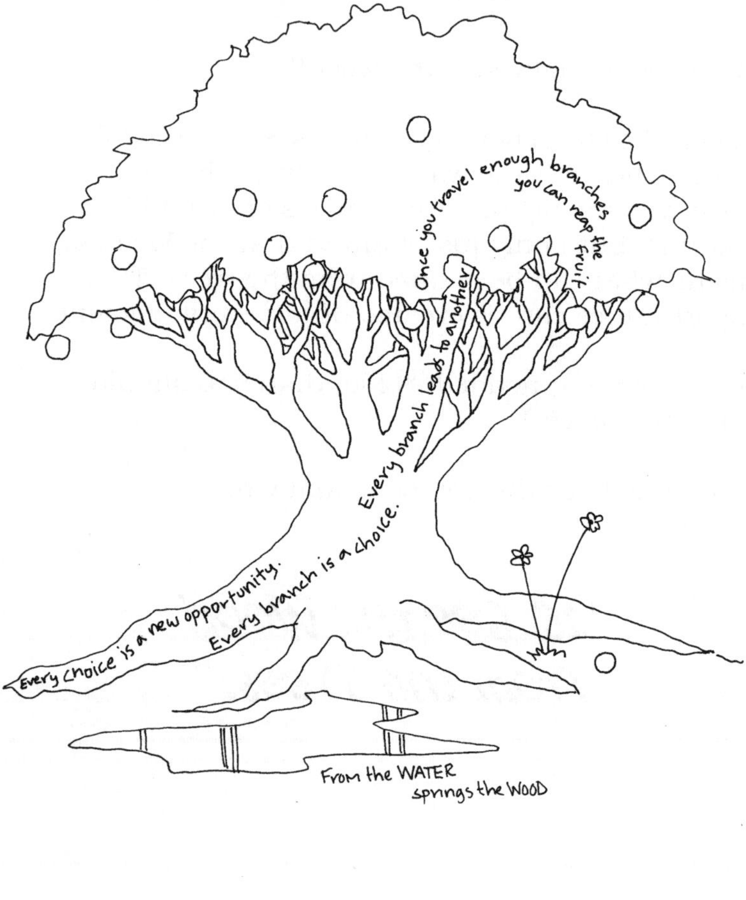

He turned back to the Fisherman. “So I’m ready to help. I’ve started to become a better carpenter. I can see the Wood for what it is. I can see that without Water the Wood can’t grow. My Dad is an amazing carpenter, and I am going to be as good as he is. He’s gifted, you know. But I’m not just going to DO better carpentry, I’m going to BE a better carpenter. I will fix up your boat, and I can learn from you to build a better ladder to my new life with my father.”

“That sounds like a fair trade, and I will be happy to oblige.” replied the Fisherman. “The going rate is $5 an hour and I have three boats. But I want you to be clear – the money you’re getting isn’t a money tap. It’s a simple time-for-money exchange – a job.

“So your real investment here is in developing your learning. But don’t wait until you start. Now that you have a vision of sorts, focus on creating that money tap, and remember opportunities lie in every moment – present, future and past.”

Rich thanked the Fisherman and walked back down to the jetty. He thought of the past opportunities of this day alone. Had he been clearer on his vision and his focus, what might have happened? Had he started with a wealth of passion and enthusiasm, what opportunities might he have uncovered?

He remembered the Fisherman’s retail stores. All that

shelving! He remembered the Gardener's bench, and all her properties – all those doors, windows, floors and skirting boards! He remembered the Plumber's maintenance franchise, and his property development company. So many opportunities for a carpenter - for a carpentry business!

There were so many opportunities to create wealth in today alone, and he had missed them all.

"You look like a man in a hurry."

Rich looked up at the Rower. "I am. I've got a lot of work to do. I've been learning, and now it's time for action. To know, and not to do, is not yet to know, you know."

"More pace, less haste," the Rower remarked.

"Pardon?"

"You need one of these." He held up one of his oars.

Rich looked at the oar, then at the Rower, and then back to the oar.

"What happened to you when you became a better rower?"

"Well, when I started rowing I learnt how to make my millions. When I became better, I learnt how to keep them. If you are in too much of a hurry, you will come back to the same place no wealthier, but exhausted all the same. There's a rhythm to wealth."

Rich was intrigued. "A rhythm to wealth?"

"When you first begin to see the wealth that is out there, you begin to see opportunities everywhere. If you don't follow a rhythm, you will either overwhelm yourself, frustrate yourself or exhaust yourself."

Rich was about to write that down when the Rower turned back to his oar. "Soon after you see wealth, you discover this."

"An oar?"

"Leverage. Put in a small amount of effort, and get out a big result. To create wealth, you need to learn how to leverage your efforts, your time and your money. You do this with other people's efforts, other people's time and other people's money."

Rich could already see this at work with the Plumber's franchise partnership, the Gardener's land financing and networking, and even how he had leveraged on the Fisherman's knowledge to catch the fish.

Rich could see how each of them couldn't have gotten the Wealth that they had without other people's efforts, time and money. It was then that he realized the true importance of the Optometrist's advice on levels of communication. Each of them had inspired the people that they met with their vision, and as a result they had created leverage. Rich wanted to leverage.

The Rower continued:

"But the key to leverage, like this oar, is that it isn't worth much if you don't know how to use it. Used in the wrong way, you'll just end up exhausting yourself with either too much or too little of the wrong people's or the right people's efforts, time and money."

Rich wrote:

"18. The key to leverage is how you use it."

The Rower pulled over a small row boat and motioned Rich to jump in. Rich took the oars and began paddling as the Rower told his story. "Soon after I began rowing I started a holiday tour company. I love the outdoors, and I had a vision of a company that would send people around the world, to the most exotic locations.

"I discovered the power of leverage, and I raised financing, recruited managers and created partnerships and agency agreements throughout the world. For five years I worked like crazy and grew the company at an incredible rate.

"It was exhausting, but I kept going. I began spending all my time on management issues and fire-fighting. We continued to raise financing and recruit staff. We were really stretched. Then the travel market hit a downturn, and we were overextended. We had creditors to pay, and payroll to meet, but the business just wasn't coming in fast enough. I burnt out. I ended up having to close the company."

Rich didn't like the sound of that at all. It didn't sound much like the Fisherman's cheerful comments about planning to fail. Then Rich realized that that was exactly what the Rower had not done. He hadn't planned to fail. In fact, if he began to fail at all – as he had - it was game over.

"It was the best thing that could have happened to me. It made me have to think about being a better rower. When I started rowing, I would be amazed at the power of this oar. But it's also difficult to manage. The harder I pulled, the more off-balance the boat became, and the slower I went. That made me try to pull even harder and spin the oar around faster to get it back in the water which, of course, wore me down even more without any results."

"When I became a better rower a strange thing happened. I found that what I was doing when the oar was out of the water was more important than when the oar was in the water."

Rich looked at the Rower as if he was a little strange. He repeated "When the oar is out of the water?"

"Your father. I'm guessing he's not leveraging much at all right now?"

"Well, no."

"That's OK. That just makes the rowing even more exhausting. Imagine your father rowing with his hands."

Rich couldn't quite picture it, but he nodded all the same.

The Rower drew a scale on Rich's notebook, from 0 to 20 and then asked "When your father is applying himself, say, to his work, how much of his full potential do you think he is applying?"

Rich stopped rowing for a moment and ringed the 6. "He's worn out most of the time, so he does work very hard, but not really at his full potential."

"OK. Now when he's not working how much, on the same scale, is he relaxed, balanced and enjoying life to the full?"

Rich cringed, and circled the 4. "His work wears him out, so when he comes home he needs to recover."

"But that's the point. If he's at a 4, he's not recovering. He's still going to be worn out when he goes back to work. So let me tell you, when you begin to leverage, all of this gets magnified by a factor of 10. When I was running my travel company, I was wearing myself down with each day. When I was rowing, I was wearing myself down with each stroke."

"Now, when I became a better rower, I learnt that the more relaxed and balanced I was when the oar was out of the water, the more prepared I was for the next stroke. That's why it's called the recovery. More importantly, the less time my oar was in the water, the faster I went. So I was spending twice as long out of the water, with half the effort, and going twice as fast."

"I now own an adventure sports company, a travel agency and a resort. I work about a week a month, and I enjoy the rest of my time travelling and living a wonderfully balanced life. When I apply myself, I apply myself fully. When I relax, I relax totally. Any challenges, I am fully able to manage. I prepare, execute, review at specific times every week and every month. It's a rhythm that makes my wealth sustainable."

Rich nodded vigorously, thinking of his father. Then he wrote:

"19. Sustainable wealth follows a rhythm."

He drew the scales he wanted to have:

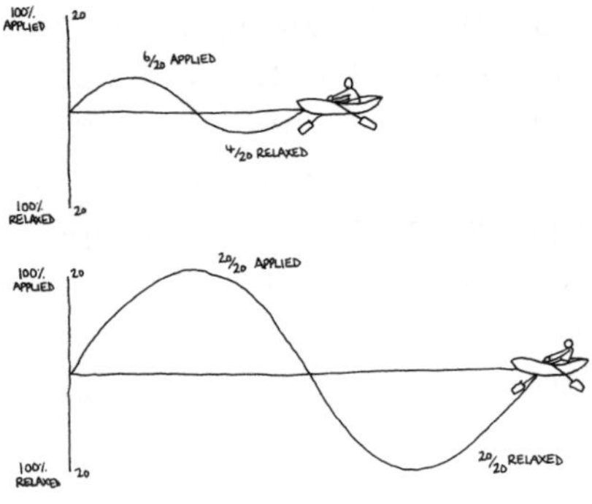

They both sat for a while, feeling the autumn breeze. The stream carried them further towards the sea. Rich thought of his father, miserably lying in bed. "So you're saying that what we do when we're not working is as important as what we do when we are?"

The Rower shook his head. "More important. When you have a vision and a focus, all your best work is done when you're not working. But remember, Rich, Wealthy people don't work. They simply follow their passion."

Rich thought about the Plumber dancing and the Gardener's picnic. It didn't seem that what they were doing would contribute to their wealth, but it would. Just by nurturing themselves, they were getting wealthier. They were relaxing at a scale 20. They would return to invest time in their investments at a scale 20. They had 20/20 vision.

He drew:

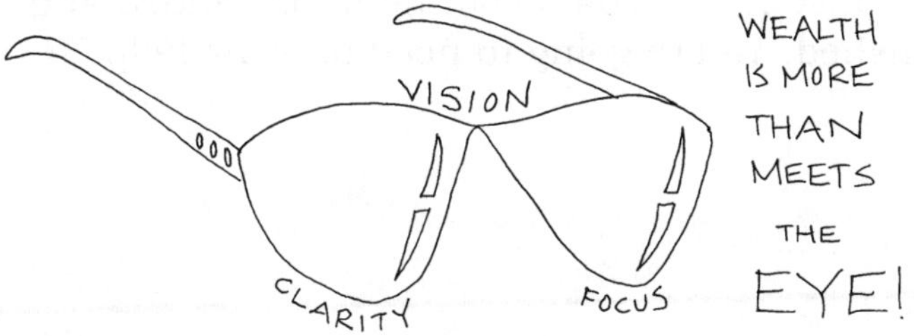

Rich heard the sound of a flute in the air. They had come to the mouth of the river, and they both looked over to a wooden gazebo on the beach. A lady was sitting, playing to the sea.

The Rower spoke to Rich. "That's the Musician. If you want to experience real wealth, I'd advise you spend some time with her."

Listening to the music, it reminded Rich of what the Gardener had said:

"11. Your passion is your compass."

Rich turned to the rower. "OK. Here's my number. I'd be happy to sand and varnish your boat for you."

The rower smiled. "Well, thank you. I have an entire boathouse full of boats waiting to be sanded and varnished. You're going to need to bring help."

Chapter 8

THE MUSICIAN

Rich stepped in to the gazebo. “Hi, I’m Rich! I have a quality wood care service and I would love to be of assistance.”

The Musician laughed. “My, you’re a young entrepreneur. Unfortunately, this gazebo isn’t mine. But my flute could do with a polish.”

Rich sat down and looked out at the sea. He had never noticed before how big it was.

“Could I tell you my vision?” Rich began.

The Musician let out a light whistle from her flute and then paused. “Draw it for me.”

And that’s what he did for the next twenty minutes, as she continued to play her flute.

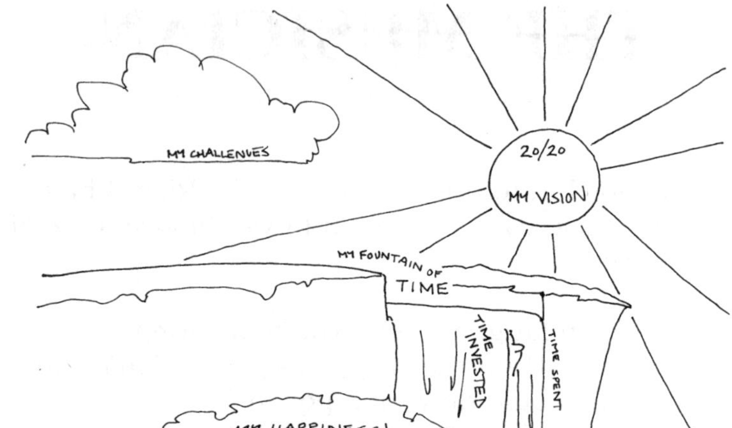
MY CHALLENGES
20/20
MY VISION
MY FOUNTAIN OF
TIME
TIME INVESTED
TIME SPENT
MY HAPPINESS!
THE FRUITS OF MY WEALTH
REINVESTED
I REAP
MY OPPORTUNITIES
MY LEARNING
MY BALANCE
MY HOME
MY HEALTH
LADDER OF LEARNING
MY ENERGY
FRIENDS
I NURTURE
INVESTORS
MENTORS
INSPIRED WORKS IN PROGRESS
MY ISLAND OF ASSETS
STAFF
SYSTEMS
PROCESSES
WOOD CARE BUSINESS
MY KNOWLEDGE
I SOW
PROPERTY INVESTMENTS
CARPENTRY FRANCHISE
MY BUSINESS PLATFORM
MY LEADERSHIP
MY PASSION
MY MINDSET
MY POOL OF WEALTH

“So now tell me why you might fail.”

Rich thought about that. It wasn’t because he would make mistakes, because he planned to fail. It wouldn’t be because he would be wasting his time or his money, because he would be investing both. It wouldn’t be because he would be moving too fast or too slow, because he would follow a rhythm.

“I don’t know. How might I fail?”

“If you were to sow in the summer, or reap in the spring. If you were to forget about...” she played her flute again “...harmony.”

She looked over at Rich, and he noticed the most incredible sparkle in her eyes.

“Tell me, Rich. What do you know about time?”

“I know that we wealthy people value it more than money. I know that we treat it very carefully because we see it as something precious. We hate to waste it.”

The Musician nodded in agreement. “Time cannot be compared to money. With money, when you spend it, you can always get more. With time, once you’ve spent it, it’s gone. It never comes back. Time is your most precious asset, so invest in understanding it better.”

Rich added that to his list:

"20. Time is your most precious asset."

Rich asked, "So what can you teach me to help me understand time better?"

The Musician looked out at the sea. "Time has flavours. Learn how to taste it, and your wealth is assured." She paused. "I'll show you. Watch the waves."

Rich looked out at the waves. They looked like every other wave he'd seen. The Musician continued, "Breathe with the wave."

Rich began to breathe in as the water line receded, and breathe out as each wave broke back up on the beach. The Musician began to play her flute, playing notes up and down the scale in time with the waves.

Rich could hear the Rower:

"19. Sustainable wealth follows a rhythm."

But this was something else. A tingle went down Rich's spine with each new wave. A peculiar thing began to happen. He was no longer just Rich. He was something much bigger. As he breathed, he became the sea, and the melody, and there became so much abundance. He suddenly saw how much more he already had, and how much more he had to give.

He thought about his father. He thought about the mother he had lost. He had blamed her for dying – for leaving him and his father. He hadn't expected to meet her again. Certainly not here and now. But his sense of oneness was overpowering.

Instead of feeling overwhelmed, he felt an incredible calm. He felt a surging inner strength well up within. The strength surged through his body, up to his chest, and up to his face, to his eyes. Rich felt an energy he could not describe. As he looked out, in harmony with some natural rhythm, he was struck by tremendous clarity.

Then he saw it. With a twinkle in his eye, he whispered "So THAT's what the World is supposed to look like..."

The Musician stopped playing, but Rich could still hear the melody. “Can you taste it?” she asked. Rich nodded. The Musician continued, “When you find true harmony, you find untold strength. Harmony is the foundation of Wealth.”

Rich quickly scribbled:

“21. Harmony is the Foundation of Wealth.”

She drew a circle:

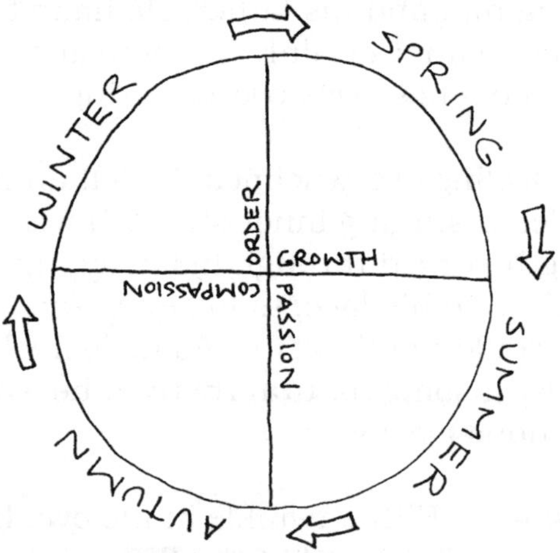

"In the sea, there are ripples on waves on currents on tides. It's the same with time. There are seasons within seasons. There is a spring, summer, autumn, winter in each year, in each day. You have seasons in your life, in your relationships, in your investments and your businesses. You have one in this journey you have taken today."

You have seasons in your learning and in your actions. Right now, you notice the seasons in your book. Your harmony gives you that knowledge.

Richard thought about that. She was right.

"When you invest your time - to sow, nurture and reap your relationships and your investments, your learning and your passion, your vision and your focus - make sure you sow in the spring, nurture in the summer and reap in the fall. It's not just what you do, it's when you do it."

Richard wrote:

"22. Time has seasons."

"23. It's not just what you do, it's when you do it."

The Musician continued:

"When you find your vision and clarity, you find your Wealth. When you find your Wealth, you can focus on how to invest your time. When you invest your time, you create value. When you create value, your wealth begins to flow. When your wealth flows with rhythm and harmony, it begins to resonate.

"Do you know what it means to resonate, Rich?"

"I felt it, but I don't understand it."

"When you resonate, you create a vibration, like ripples in a pond. You create the most wonderful attraction – you attract the best people, the best opportunities, the best environment. That's when you really begin to live life fully. When you resonate, you accumulate."

Rich was reminded of the birds and butterflies in the Gardener's garden. He wrote:

"24. When you resonate, you accumulate."

The sun was moving lower in the sky, and the air was beginning to cool. Rich looked at the Musician. He hadn't asked her how wealthy she was, but he realized he didn't need to. He could see the wealth in her entire body. He asked:

"Is that how you became so wealthy? You attracted everything to you?"

The Musician shook her head. "The attraction isn't the cause. It's the effect. When you begin to attract wonderful things, that's just the clue that you're on the right track. If you are not, that's a sign to re-calibrate. The attraction is the reward you get for your efforts."

"No, when I became a better musician, I developed clarity about when and where to create new investments, when to build them, when to sell them. I became a master of my time and my focus by just being in tune with the market and with my advisors. I came across the secret of all great wealth."

"What's the secret?"

"That's for you to find out."

"Can you give me a clue?"

The Musician smiled, and then began to play the same melody she had been playing earlier. Rich looked back out at the sea.

In mid-melody, the Musician abruptly stopped.

The melody continued in Rich's mind.

She turned to Rich. "I began to know which note came next."

Rich looked at her quizzically, and another tune came into his head:

"The World is waiting,
Anticipating..."

Rich saw his reflection in her smiling blue eyes. His reflection was twinkling. As he held her gaze, the Musician winked.

Chapter 9

THE INN KEEPER

Rich and the Musician walked along the beach, towards a beautiful resort. As they approached, a very large man came out to greet them. The Musician spoke to Rich;

"This is one of the resorts in the Rower's resort chain. This is the Inn Keeper. He'll get you back home. But first, you should spend some time with him."

Rich replied "You mean invest some time with him?"

The Musician grinned "Yes, invest!"

The Inn Keeper welcomed Rich with a grizzly bear handshake and a wrestler's hug. "You must be Rich! Welcome to my paradise! Please come in."

Rich entered the resort to find the most astounding gardens, fountains and fish ponds. The ambience was totally relaxing, and the hotel staff seemed to drift along like they were wearing magic carpet shoes.

“I met the Gardener today, and your gardens are almost as beautiful as hers. She has the most amazing vision you know. ”

The Inn Keeper sighed. “Ah yes, I had a friend who had a vision even bigger than the Gardener’s.”

“You do? Who is she?”

“Oh, she’s just a nobody. Never made anything of her life. Just gets by.”

Rich wasn’t expecting that. “Does she know what it takes to get wealthy? Has she met the Plumber, and the Fisherman? Has she met the Musician?”

“Oh, sure she has. She just never made it like they did.”

The sun was beginning to set, and Rich suddenly felt an indescribable fear. What if he woke up tomorrow and everything was an illusion? What if things weren’t as clear as they had seemed on the beach? Then he remembered the Musician’s eyes, and he asked a better question:

“Why didn’t she make it?”

"Because she was happy to settle for less. You know, I was too, until I became a better Inn Keeper."

Rich waited expectantly.

"You know, I love to serve people. I love to give people a wonderful experience, especially when that is what they have specifically come for. I always wanted to do my best. I do that in my job, and I do that every day in my life. But in the past, my standards were low."

"How could your standards be low if you were doing your best?"

The Inn Keeper sat down on an elegant settee and Rich followed. A waiter came up with two fruit cocktails. "Have you ever been to a three star hotel?"

Rich thought about it "I've been inside the two star hotel in the village."

"Were the people working there doing their best?"

"Yes, they were."

"And did you have the same experience as you are having here?"

"No, of course not!" Rich paused. An entirely new clarity began to form.

The Inn Keeper continued, "For a long time, I always felt I tried my best, but I never seemed to get anywhere. I began to invest my time in developing myself. I learnt many of the keys to wealth, but wealth still eluded me. It was then that I realized I was still living a two star life.

"Even though I knew I should be investing my time, I continued to spend it. Even though I knew I should be building a better plumbing system, I kept putting it off. Even though I knew there was a rhythm to wealth, I never looked hard enough for it. I was still doing my best, but ultimately I was willing to settle for less."

Rich interrupted "So how did you become a better Inn Keeper?"

"I raised my standards. You see, it isn't your knowledge that will make you wealthy, it is what you do with that knowledge."

Rich remembered what the Fisherman had said:

"12. To know and not to do, is not yet to know."

"When I raised my standards, I was no longer willing to settle for spending my time. I was no longer willing to settle for a mediocre life. I was no longer willing to settle for a sloppy mind and blurred vision. When you no longer settle for certain behaviour, you have no option but to take action and change it.

"So the life we live is not determined by the life we want to live tomorrow, but by the life we settle for today. We settle for our standards."

Rich wrote:

"25. You settle for your standards."

"Now, Rich. Here's a secret for you."

Rich leaned in, spilling some of his fruit cocktail.

"Did the Musician tell you about attraction?"

Rich nodded.

"If you're running a two star hotel, what kind of people are you going to attract?"

Rich answered “Two star people?”

“And if you’re running a five star hotel?”

Rich got the picture.

“And here’s another secret.” The Inn Keeper swept his hand as if he was sowing seeds on the marble floor. “Five star is about service, quality and conduct. These things don’t cost money. It just takes better rules and better systems to ensure you don’t settle for less. So higher standards do not need to cost more and, in fact...”

He leaned in, and Rich leaned also.

“...Who do you think has to put in more effort? The man with the two star life or the man with the five star life?”

Rich thought about the people he knew who wanted more but were willing to settle for less. He thought about his father. He thought about the people he had met today. There was no question:

“The man with the two star life has to put in a lot more effort.” And he wrote that down:

"26. A Five Star life is easier than a Two Star life."

Rich was inspired again, and he wrote his list of five star rules and systems.

Then he came up with a question for the Inn Keeper. "Now that you are living a five star life, why do you choose to work for the Rower instead of working for yourself?"

The Inn Keeper erupted with laughter. "I love my work! Don't take that away from me! I do what I love for a living, I live in my paradise expense-free, and all my earnings are taken care of by a wonderful money plumbing system. Wealth has given me the freedom to choose, and this is what I choose. This is my vision of the perfect life."

The Inn Keeper sat up. "Now, Rich, I have a question for you. If you were to put me in a two star environment, what do you think would happen? Would I go back to living a two star life?"

Rich thought the answer was obvious. "No, you would either change the environment or go back to an environment that was five star, because you wouldn't settle for less."

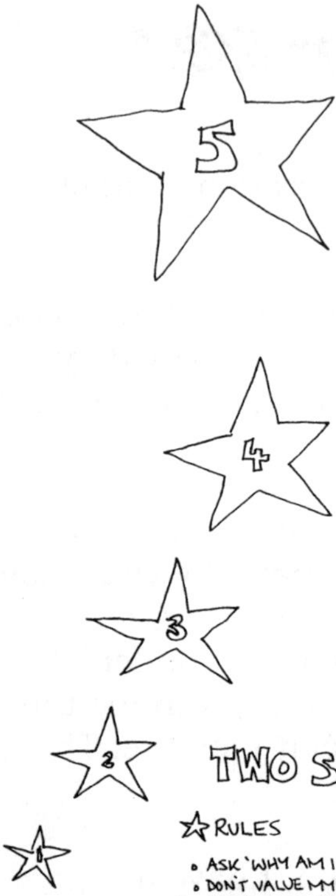

FIVE STAR

RULES

- ASK 'HOW CAN I BUILD ON THE WEALTH I HAVE ALREADY CREATED?
- ASK 'HOW CAN I CREATE VALUE FOR OTHERS?
- ASK 'WHAT WEALTH HAVE I CREATED TODAY?
- VALUE MY TIME MORE THAN MONEY, AND MEASURE HOW MUCH I INVEST EACH WEEK
- VALUE MYSELF AS MY GREATEST ASSET, AND SEE MYSELF GROW WITH EVERY NEW DAY I INVEST IN MYSELF, MY LEARNING, MY NETWORK AND MY BUSINESSES
- FOLLOW THE RHYTHM OF WEALTH AND SENSE WHEN I'M WORKING TOO HARD AND GOING TO SLOW
- TASTE MY TIME AND TASTE MY VISION DAILY
- USE MY PASSION AS MY COMPASS

SYSTEMS

- MANAGE MY TIME BY INVESTING AN INCREASING AMOUNT WEEK BY WEEK ON VALUE IN LINE WITH MY VISION
- MANAGE MY NETWORK BY INVESTING TIME WITH PEOPLE WHO SHARE MY PASSION AND MY VISION, AND BY INVESTING MY TIME WITH PEOPLE WHO INSPIRE AND MOTIVATE ME
- MANAGE MY LEARNING BY FOCUSING DAILY ON WHAT I NEED TO LEARN MOST TO ALLOW ME TO ADD VALUE IN LINE WITH MY VISION

DIRECTION
PLUS
DISCIPLINE
EQUALS
DECISIVENESS

TWO STAR

RULES

- ASK 'WHY AM I NOT WEALTHY?'
- DON'T VALUE MY TIME AND SPEND IT FREELY
- DON'T VALUE MYSELF AND SPEND ON THE OUTSIDE INSTEAD OF INVESTING ON THE INSIDE
- BLAME THE ENVIRONMENT
- WEAR MYSELF DOWN TRYING
- USE MY EMOTIONS AS MY COMPASS

SYSTEMS

- MANAGE MY TIME BY DOING WHAT NEEDS TO BE DONE FOR MY JOB OR MY RELIEF
- MANAGE MY TIME WITH MY NETWORK BY SPENDING IT WITH PEOPLE I ALREADY KNOW
- MANAGE MY LEARNING BY SEEING WHAT STRIKES ME DAY BY DAY

AMBITION
MINUS
FOCUS
EQUALS
FRUSTRATION

The Inn Keeper nodded. "So what will you do when you go back to your environment tonight?"

Rich sat in silence.

"Remember, Rich, you become your choices. All your choices and your learning will be made in your environment. If learning is a game, your environment is your playground. Don't settle for less."

Rich wrote:

"27. Your environment is your playground."

"28. You are the result of your choices."

It was getting dark. Rich thought back to the choice he took when he followed the overgrown path, and as a result of that choice, who he had now become. As the Inn Keeper drove him home, he thought about what he would tell his father. He thought about what the Optician had said:

"2. Choose the level you want to play at."

In all the nine years of his life, the only level of communication he had known with his father was exchange and connect. Tonight, he was going to inspire.

Chapter 10

THE CARPENTER

He was home! Rich ran excitedly to his front door, gripping on to his notebook as he opened the door. His heart was pumping and a big grin was stamped on his face.

Rich ran through the house and opened his father's bedroom door.

"Dad, we're going to be rich! You won't believe what happened today!"

"Richard! Why have you been out for so long? Where's the Well Water?"

Richard stopped dead. "Oh. No, I didn't get the Well Water. But look what I did get." He held out the notebook.

The Carpenter pulled himself up in bed and looked at Richard in despair. "Richard, where is the Well Water? That's all you had to do today. Go to the Well of Wealth and get the Water. We need the Water, Richard. Where's the Water?"

Richard pleaded “No Dad, we don’t need that Well Water. The Well of Wealth isn’t where you think it is. I’ve seen the ocean, Dad. I’ve seen the ocean.”

Richard saw his father’s eyes well up, as the Carpenter shook his head. He slowly pulled himself from the bed and began to put on his socks. “I have to go. I have to go now to the Well. We have to get the Water.”

“Dad, it’s night time. Do it in the morning. Dad, time is so precious. Let me tell you my vision. Let me tell you what I’ve learnt today.” His words were falling about him, dropping on the floor before they reached the ears of the Carpenter.

“Where’s the dollar, Richard?”

The words came out like they were causing the Carpenter pain, and he doubled up as he stood. Richard began to cry.

“I’m sorry. I don’t have the dollar anymore.”

“Oh, Richard. You have no idea. This is terrible. This is so terrible. What have you done.” The old man shuffled to the money box, pulling out a dollar and pulling on his coat. “I have to go now. I have to get to the Well. Lock the door after me. I’ve got keys.”

Richard began to cry harder as the Carpenter laboured towards the door.

"No, Dad. Please. Please let me tell you. Look at my notebook. Look at what I've written. Please, Dad. Look. Learning is a game. Time is our most precious asset. Dad, it's all here. Please just sit for a minute and let me explain it to you."

Richard desperately wiped his eyes. His tears were washing away his vision, washing away his clarity.

"Let me inspire you. The Well is right here. The Well is in your Words."

He was talking to a closed door.

He sat on the floor and began to cry. He started thinking about his mum, and that made him cry even more. This was going to be his best day, and now it was his worst day. It was like a bad dream. None of it was real. Only his tears were real. His tears, and his father's pain, and the cold floor.

As Richard lay there like a broken puppet, crying himself to sleep, the words of the Musician floated into his mind:

"23. It's not just what you do, it's when you do it."

And the winter passed.

Chapter 11

THE OLD LADY

"It's just not fair!"
"I am sick and tired."

And he was. Both sick and tired. In fact, he was tired of being sick and sick of being tired. Was it fair? Rich's father had worked all his life as a Carpenter. He had always wanted wealth but had never received it. That drove him to work even harder, and the pressure had finally squashed him flat.

He was flat broke, and flat on his back in bed.

Rich was by his side. "Dad, I'm sorry about yesterday. Something wonderful happened which I'll tell you all about later. But today, I promise to visit the Well of Wealth for you."

The Carpenter smiled. "Thanks, son. I'm sorry I upset you last night. But you can't miss a day, so I had to go. It's better to be safe than sorry."

Then, giving him a dollar, he said:

"For centuries, people in this village have made it a habit to visit the Well of Wealth every day without fail. Give generously to the Well, my son, and it will give generously in return."

Rich took the dollar and practically ran with the notebook up the path to the Well. He soon came to the Old Lady who was, again, sitting with a glass of chilled water in her hands.

"My, you're looking Rich today!" she exclaimed.

"I came back to say thank you, and to get your number. I'm starting a Carpentry and Wood Care Business, and I'm going to ask the Plumber for some advice on what I need to do to franchise it later. Then I want to speak to the Rower about serving all the boats on the river. I'd like to have a workshop at his Boathouse."

"Well, well, well. That sounds just fine," said the Old Lady. "And have you been making good use of that notebook?"

"Oh, yes, thank you." He showed her the picture of his list.

1 Think it Ink it Do it Review it
2 Choose the level you want to PLAY at.
3 What you SEE Is always What you GET
4 Ask and you Shall Receive
5 LEARNING is a GAME
Invest more of your time Spend less of it 6
Invest more of your money Spend less of it 7
8 YOUR WELL IS IN YOUR WORDS
9 Wealth is the Beginning Not the end
10 SOW NURTURE REAP
N
E
S
W
11 YOUR PASSION IS YOUR COMPASS
12
To know and not to do is not yet to know
13 Value is the river in which wealth flows
14 Become an inspired WORK-IN-PROGRESS
15 PLAN TO FAIL
16 SEE THE WOOD FROM THE TREES
17 OPPORTUNITIES lie in every MOMENT
What else have you not yet seen?
18 The KEY to leverage is how you use it
19 Sustainable wealth follows a rhythm
20 TIME IS your most precious ASSET
21 HARMONY is the foundation of wealth
22 TIME HAS SEASONS
GO
STOP
23 It's not just what you do. It's when you do it
24 When you resonate you accumulate
25 You settle for your standards
26 A FIVE STAR life is easier than A THREE STAR life
27 Your environment is your playground..
28 You are the result of your CHOICES

“Very good. Now, before you are on your way, do you have any better questions for me?”

“Yes, I do. First of all, I need to find the Well of Wealth, where I can get a bucket of water for my father. Which way is it?”

“Do you have a better question?”

Rich objected “I really need to get to the Well, or my father will be very upset.”

“So, do you have a better question?’

Rich thought for a while. Then he looked back at his list.

“How many more are there on this list?”

The Old Lady smiled. “Two, for now.”

Rich nodded. “And should I have learnt them already?”

The Old Lady continued smiling, and nodded.

Rich began to think about the last day. He sat down by the Old Lady and he thought hard, because he also knew he was missing something. And it was something very big.

He felt it had something to do with the type of people he had met. He felt there was something to do with how they were connected. He knew it had something to do with the Musician's melody and the little girl's song:

"The World is Waiting,
Anticipating..."

Rich thought harder. He looked at the water in the Old Lady's hand. She hadn't drunk it, and it reminded him again of the Water from the Well of Wealth. It made him think of the water in the fountain, in the garden. It made him think of the water in the river and in the sea.

He thought very hard about the water, and what each person he had met was doing with it. All that everyone in the village seemed to do with the Water from the Well was to drink it.

But everyone he met yesterday seemed to value the water in a different way. It seemed that the last thing they needed to worry about was having enough to drink. They found the value in a different way – but also in a much bigger way.

He knew that there was something here he needed to understand. Through his journey yesterday, there was always more water than he could possibly use, and it kept getting bigger and bigger. He remembered what the Optician had said:

"3. What you see is always what you get."

Then he thought about the panic in his father last night when he didn't have the Well Water, and his mood suddenly changed. The Old Lady seemed to know what Rich was thinking, and she whispered

"Water, water, everywhere. And not a drop to drink."

Rich began to gain further clarity. He nodded towards the glass of water. "So what is that for?"

"Few are like you, Rich. Few come asking to be wealthy. Many people come to me looking for the Well of Wealth, so I point them to the Well. But wouldn't you know, most don't even ask that. They come and simply tell me they are thirsty."

"To those people, I give the glass of water."

"Once they have quenched their thirst, they don't take either path. They simply turn around and go back home."

The Old Lady looked at Rich, and he looked back. He thought about the glass, the bucket and the sea. She nodded towards his notebook, and he wrote:

"29. Water always finds its level."

The Old Lady looked at Rich with a twinkle, and said, "Then this is all you'll be needing for your father." She handed him an empty bucket from the Well of Wealth.

Rich squinted in comprehension. "So you own the Well of Wealth."

"I sure do. Wealthiest girl in the village."

"But it's not the real Well..." Rich continued.

The Old Lady sighed. "We all own that well, Rich. But my vision is to help those who really don't want to help themselves. The Well of Wealth can't give them wealth, but it can give them security. This glass can't give security, but it can give relief. Succeed, sustain or survive. It's all a matter of choice."

It was true. Anyone could have made the journey Rich had made yesterday. Most didn't because they weren't willing to invest the necessary time to succeed. It was their choice. Rich remembered what the Inn Keeper had said:

"28. You are the result of your choices."

"Then why did you help me?"

"Because you asked. And I sent you to the person who had the right vision."

"The Optometrist. I never did find out his vision."

The Old Lady smiled, "Yes, you did."

Rich smiled back, then nodded. He looked at her with a better question. "So what comes after No. 29?"

"If you don't see it, you know the answer. What you see is always what you get."

The Old Lady confided, "But Rich, I will tell you this. Never give up the search for what comes next, because one day you will find it. When you find it, you will realize that whilst the Well of Wealth springs from our Words, what comes next is Wealth beyond Words."

What was he missing? What came after No. 29? He knew this was the one. He knew this was the biggest one by far.

He could sense the connection between the people he had met. Or maybe it was the sequence. He thought hard about their words. He wasn't seeing something in their words.

He was going to have to become a better carpenter.

Something in his list of 29 was wrong. The order was wrong. He needed to change the steps in the ladder. He was going to have to think it, ink it, do it, review it.

When he had promised the Old Lady he would work hard, he hadn't realized it would be this hard.

What came after No. 29? It seemed the answer lay behind him. But as he would have to re-read his book, the answer really lay ahead of him. He was determined not to settle for less. He would re-read his book until he could see the answer.

Rich breathed in the crisp, spring air, and knew he had been here before. It had been only a day, or was it a month? Or a year?

He felt greater clarity, and looked again at the Old Lady.

What came after No. 29?

The Old Lady looked back with eyes of cool blue.

They were young eyes, full of spirit. Rich saw humour and fun dancing in those wonderful pools. Her eyes reminded him of the fountain the plumber was dancing in. They reminded him of the river the girls were swimming in. What came after No. 29?

As he stared into her eyes, transfixed, he became aware of time. He could feel the flow of time like the rush of water past the boat.

As he looked into the blue, the current calmed, and he could see the sparkling ocean. His precious time slowed to a lazy sway, and then came to a stop.

He held his breath.

With a twinkle in her eye, she winked.

And finally, he saw it.

THE END

"The World is waiting,
Anticipating..."

Afterword

Welcome back, and thank you for reading this book.

Please be advised that this is not an ordinary story. The real story isn't in the story. The real story is a magical story behind the story, waiting to be revealed. That means it only comes out to play in a repeat reading. Whether that's in the fifth reading or the fifteenth reading is up to you.

The real story is waiting, holding out the keys to your own personal wealth.

If you have not yet discovered the real story in this book, are you ready to settle for that? Or are you ready to work harder?

We settle for our standards. Is your standard the glass full that you receive from the first few times you read this story, the first few times you discuss it, or will you only settle for the ocean?

Each time you read this story, your clarity and your focus will increase. What you see is always what you get. As you see more, you will get more. Eventually, as your level increases, you will get the ocean. Water will always find its level.

If you want more than simply a glass full, the answer comes in thinking it and inking it. If you already know that to know and not to do is not yet to know, then where is your pen? What have you been inking? What have you been doing?

If you want more clarity, then ask better questions. Question your assumptions.

What does each advisor have in common other than the obvious? What is your definition of wealth?

Why is their sequence important to wealth creation and why is their sequence not necessarily in the right order? What is the right order?

How does rearranging the order of Rich's list get you closer to what comes after No. 29?

What was the Optometrist's vision?

If the real story isn't the story, what is the real story? If what you see is what you get, what are you still not seeing?

What doors are you not opening? Better questions are keys that question and open doors that you had stopped questioning and closed.

There are two better questions that will get you closer, faster, to the real story. Questions that question your assumptions:

If the water throughout the story does not represent what you assume it does, what does it really represent?

And if Rich's journey did not take the day you assume it took, how long did it take? How long will it take?

We settle for our standards. Is your standard the glass full that you receive from the first few times you read this story, the first few times you discuss it, or will you only settle for the ocean. Will you actually think it, ink it, do it, review it?

You are the result of your choices.

So please use this story as you would a watering can. The more you sprinkle it, the more you grow.

Directions for use:

Apply
Rinse
Repeat

The beginning is in the end.

"It takes courage to grow up and become who you really are."

E.G. Cummings

WEALTH DYNAMICS

The Wealth Dynamics profiling system was developed in 2000 by Roger Hamilton. Wealth Dynamics provides an intuitive system which equips an entrepreneur with:

1. Clarity on their path of least resistance to success
2. One of eight paths with a list of identifiable role models and biographies
3. A six step process to building the right team and focusing on the right activity
4. Links to the growth stages in business, giving clarity on leadership succession
5. Links to country, industry and lifestyle trends, giving clarity on when losing formulas become winning formulas.

Wealth Dynamics is an evolution of Jungian psychometric testing into specific action and thinking dynamics that relates to entrepreneurs. It goes back to the roots of personality profiling in Chinese philosophy which precedes Western psychometric testing by 2,500 years.

To discover more about Wealth Dynamics visit **www.resultsfoundation.com** or **www.wealthdynamics.org** where you will find information on upcoming events, and be able to discover your own "Wealth profile" and path of least resistance by taking the online "wealth profiling" test.

ABOUT ROGER

Roger Hamilton is Asia' Leading Wealth Consultant. In the last 12 months he has shared powerful wealth creation principles with over 30,000 people in more than 150 conferences, seminars and workshops.

After graduating from Trinity College, Cambridge in Architecture, Roger decided to become a better architect, which he interpreted as building enterprises, teams, value and wealth, rather than apartment blocks and shopping malls.

Roger became a serial entrepreneur, failing many times before becoming a millionaire in his late twenties and retiring at the age of thirty. Now, in his retirement he has committed himself to a vision of World Wide Wealth: Studying and teaching the concept of making money to give away.

Now, he owns twelve businesses in publishing, design, property, event management, franchising, training and resort management. He currently resides in Bali and Singapore and conducts seminars and coaching in all corners of the world.

He is the Chairman of XL Group and XL Results Foundation, Asia's largest entrepreneur network. He is also the publisher of XL Magazine, the firstv magazine dedicated to Social Enterprise.

For recent media articles, and Roger's schedule, visit **www.rogerhamilton.com**

ROGER HAMILTON'S ENTREPRENEUR EVENTS

The following events take place in various countries:

ENTREPRENEUR BUSINESS SCHOOL
Entrepreneurship in Action

Held in Bali twice every year, the Entrepreneur Business School is a combination of a business plan competition and a course in entrepreneurship.

Join in a high profile mentor panel and entrepreneurs from around the world in an amazing and intense five days focused at what it takes to build a successful business.

Leave with an in-depth appreciation of effective business strategies, and an international network to support your growth.

WEALTH DYNAMICS WEEKEND
Financial Flight School to Accelerated Wealth

The Wealth Dynamics Weekend is Roger's Cornerstone Program. What happens to you at the Weekend is what happens to Rich in this book. Through a highly interactive program of learning, networking, activities and games, you will gain in invaluable insight into your own wealth psychology.

You will discover your path of least resistance through Roger's ground breaking Wealth Dynamics profiling system, together with a step-by-step plan to build your wealth by following your passion.

The emphasis is on action. An average of 20 to 30 businesses are created as a result of each event with individuals, having gained clarity on their path, attracting the right management teams, financing, peers and mentors.

For more information on these events, visit:
www.resultsfoundation.com

WORLD WIDE WEALTH

World Wide Wealth : Empowering social enterprise and global change by increasing our collective ability to create and contribute wealth.

Wealth isn't how much money you have, but what you are left with if you lose all your money. It can be measured by contribution. As we create more wealth, we should see this translate into a richer environment on this planet when we leave than when we arrived.

World Wide Wealth is the promise of individual and collective wealth. It is the promise of an end to poverty. This is our vision... this is the vision of the Optometrist. This is our vision and we invite you to make it yours.

www.resultsfoundation.com

The Billion Dollar Challenge, launched throughout Asia Pacific in 2006, supports the vision of World Wide Wealth. The Billion Dollar Challenge has been introduced to encourage entrepreneurs to share their knowledge, skills and resources with like minded socially conscious entrepreneurs to generate greater individual and collective success. The Billion Dollar Challenge has set an annual target of generating a billion dollars in new wealth each year through the participating social enterprises, with at least 10% ($100m) being contributed directly by each company to their nominated charity.

XL RESULTS FOUNDATION

XL Results Foundation is the force behind World Wide Wealth.

LIFE MEMBERSHIP: THE POWER TO CREATE AND CONTRIBUTE

XL Results Foundation has built a powerful suite of services to enable you to accelerate the learning, network and business success of entrepreneurs world wide. Every XL Life Member is a stakeholder in this unique enterprise – and enjoy the following benefits:

ENTREPRENEUR SEMINARS

Deep discounts and often free admission to accelerate your learning.

XL Results Foundation runs large scale seminars for entrepreneurs globally, including the Global Entrepreneurs Summit featuring the Social Entrepreneur of the Year Award, and Roger Hamilton's Series of seminars: The Wealth Dynamics Weekend and The Entrepreneur Business School.

NETWORKING EVENTS

Free admission and a warm welcome to all networking events for life.

You will be able to find the partners, financiers, mentors and team members you are looking for in any of the 16 countries where XL Results Foundation run regular networking evenings. Country representatives will support you with introductions at these events in every country.

ONLINE CONNECTIONS
Free entry and facilitated introductions into our exclusive XL Life Member groups online.

Tap into a worldwide resource base to find who and what you want, where you want, when you want. We manage the largest online business directory and online business forum in the region: Join our XL Group on LinkedIn (The World's largest online business directory); and on Ecademy (The World's most popular online business forum), with access to over 2,000 industry & regional forums, 50,000 entrepreneurs and over 200 monthly networking events in 151 countries.

COACHING & MENTORING
Gain certification and advanced certification in life coaching and professional mentorship.

Attend the certification modules in Life Coaching and Wealth Consulting and get certified to earn from your knowledge. This is exclusive to Life Members, as Life Members provide XL Results Foundation with the coaching and speaker expertise we need to build World Wide Wealth. Repeat modules at any time, in any country, for life.

XL ACCREDITATION
Facilitate World Wide Wealth by coaching and consulting our accredited social enterprises.

LIFE MEMBERS

XL Results Foundation has established the first Social Enterprise standard and accreditation program for businesses. Social Entrepreneurs carrying the approved Social Enterprise Seal through this accreditation enjoy the recognition of socially responsible consumers and partners. Our Life Members are able to provide expert assistance to support these companies.

PUBLICATIONS

Receive free subscription to the latest advice and stories from the best entrepreneurs and advisors in the World.

XL Magazine is the world's first international magazine dedicated to Social Enterprise. The mix of advice from entrepreneurs and experts from around the world are available both in the magazine and online. Roger Hamilton's Online Newsletter provides regular inspiration and advice for entrepreneurs and professionals and reaches 40,000 each month.

Life Members support the growth of World Wide Wealth, and in the process grow their own personal wealth. They are our elite support team and they are our success stories. XL Life Membership is limited in each country and is transferable. Price is on application.

ACKNOWLEDGEMENTS

I would like to thank the following for their part in creating an inspired work-in-progress. Without their assistance, this book may still have been published, but it would be full of blank pages:

Renate, Kathleen, Theresa and Luke – my wonderful wife and children

Abu Hanifah, Adam Khoo, Albert Lu, Albert Einstein, Alex Tamilvanan, Andrea Gutwirth, Andrew Grant, Andrew Harris, Andrew Tan, Andri Haris Foe, Angela Ip, Anthony Robbins, Alan Kleiner, Alan Ong, Albert Lam, Arun, Aw Joo Lee, Ayrton Senna, Bernie Utchenik, Bob Denton, Bob Urichuck, Brad Pitt, Bruce Lee, Carlos Rios, Carol Broadhurst, Carolyn Boddington, Cecilia Yeung, Celine Ong, Charles Schultz, Chiaharu Kumarjima, Chris Koh, Chris Sutherst, Chrystean Tan, Christina Tan, Curtis Montgomery, DC Cordova, Dale Gerstenslager, Dale Raynes, Daryl Bisset, Dave Rogers, David Beckham, David Brent, David Ho, David Pang, Dawn Ng, Deborah Law, Deli Abedi, Dennis Wee, Desley Truscott, Dewi Kartika Joe, Dolly Yeo, Donatus Michalka, Doug Callandar, Edwin Cheung, Elaine Hamilton, Ella Grundy, Emily Kok, Emma Hamilton, Flora Hamilton, Floyd Cowan, Faudziah Utchenik, Freddie Mercury, Gary Larson, Gill Daldin, Glen Watkins, Goh Kim Siew, Graeme Fowler, Harrison Ford, Holly Grundy, Homer Simpson, Ian Grundy, Inga Carson, Irene Millar, Jacklyn Lim, Jacqui Allard, Jamie Paton, Janet Dougherty, Jasmine Lu, Jasmine Tan, Jen Mackenzie, Jennifer Lopez, Jenny Goh, Jenny Greenhalgh, Jerome Tan, Jessica Yap, John Cleese, Jorva Hamilton, Joseph Campbell, Katherine Tan, Kathy Zhang, Keanu Reaves, Ken Blanchard, Kevin Heppleston, Khevitha Kamal, Khoon Sau Lin, Kinzie, KK Ralhan, Lawrence Lee, Leng Lundemo, Lew Ko Ming, Lim Geok Khoon, Linda Chandler, Lisa McCarthy, Luke Skywalker, Markus Karlsson, Mandy Rigger, Marcus Luer, Margaret Loh, Marilyn Chua, Mark Littlewood, Mark Thorburn, Martin Hamilton, Martin Hayes, Martin Slagter, Matthew Faid, Matthias Gelber, Melissa Kang, Merrin Pearse, Michael Braunstein, Michael Dell, Mike Doyle, Mike Handcock, Mike Ross, Mary Lim, Muhammed Ali, Moshe Gerstenhaber, Muhamad Azlin Bin Ismail, Neil Hamilton, Nicole Kidman, Norman Foster, Nursyahirah Bte AB Rahman, Ong Khia Wee, Paul Dunn, Penny Power, Penny Wee, Pete Citron, Peter Harkness, Peter Kwok, Peter Watkins, Philip Sohn, Poonam Sagar, Randy Gage, Ranjan Marwah, Rebecca Bisset, Rhoda M, Richard Branson, Richard Rogers,

ACKNOWLEDGEMENTS

Richard Tan, Ricky Ang, Robert Kiyosaki, Ron Kaufman, Rory Hamilton, Scott Friedman, Shahida Hamzah, Shinta Waters, Soh Geok Leng, Stephen Dale, Stephen Hawkins, Stephen Tay, Steven Chow, Steven Khong, Steven Spielberg, Steven Tan, Sue Clark, Suzanne Braunstein, Sylvia Hii, Tan Bee Bee, Tania Tan, The Rock, Thomas Edison, Tim Hansen, Tracy Perkins, Tracie Pangrazio, Tom Hopkins, Thomas Power, Valerie Trevor, Veronica Akiew, Veronica Tan, Vivienne Bryers, Wendy Kwek, William Durran, Will Smith, William Gates, Winston Lau, Wong Seng Hon, Yenny Wong, Yap Keong Foon, Yoda, Zaharil Bin Ismail, and all our XL Life Members.